THE HIDDEN ORDER

Tokyo through the Twentieth Century

Yoshinobu Ashihara

Translated and adapted by
Lynne E. Riggs

Introduction by
Daniel J. Boorstin

Foreword by
Edward T. Hall

KODANSHA INTERNATIONAL
Tokyo・New York・London

Back cover illustration: As in Mandelbrot's fractal geometry, apparent chaos embraces a flexible order.

Originally published in Japanese, in 1986, under the title *Kakureta chitsujo*, by Chūōkōron-sha, Tokyo.

Distributed in the United States by Kodansha America, Inc., 114 Fifth Avenue, New York, NY 10011, and in the United Kingdom and continental Europe by Kodansha Europe Ltd., Gillingham House, 38-44 Gillingham Street, London SW1V 1HU. Published by Kodan-sha International Ltd., 17-14 Otowa 1-chome, Bunkyo-ku, Tokyo 112, and Kodansha America, Inc.

First published, 1989.
First paperback edition, 1992

92 93 94 95 96 10 9 8 7 6 5 4 3 2 1

ISBN 4-7700-1664-6   LCC 88-81847

CONTENTS

INTRODUCTION

There is perhaps no area where the distinctive
Japanese experience has had a more visible influence
on the West than in architecture. Western enthusiasts
and admirers of Japanese culture, including some of
our best Western architects, have attempted to import
or adapt features, or even styles, of Japanese architecture to the West. Yoshinobu Ashihara, a brilliant prac-
ticing architect, and a citizen of the whole architectural
world, helps us understand why some efforts have been
more successful than others, and provides us a guide to
the enlightened borrowing of Japanese ways of architecture.

This book, more cogently than any other I know,
shows us how the mainstream of the Japanese architectural tradition has been shaped by the shores along
which it has flowed. Mr. Ashihara shows us how the
Japanese house—its materials, its orientation, its
design, its aesthetic—has been shaped by the climate,
the history, and the ways of daily life in Japan. With a
poetic insight, he contrasts the sharp outlines of
Western architecture, on the stony wall-dominated
Parthenon-model, and its antithesis of light and
darkness, against the Japanese world of shadows, of
the horizontal view, in its floor-oriented realm of

wood. He contrasts the Western architecture of the whole, the distant view, the frontal symmetry, with the Japanese architecture of the parts, the love of detail enchanted with texture and immersed in nature. The flow of inside and outside, which came naturally to Japan, in the West had to await the perfection of glass.

Mr. Ashihara's remarkable feat in this book is that while he shows us how thoroughly Japanese architecture is a product of Japan, at the same time he gives us a newly subtle grasp on the relevance of these characteristic Japanese ways to architects in the West. His discovery of the hidden order in the Japanese townscape begins with the familiar Japanese custom of removing shoes on entering a house. He leads us gradually to some of the largest features of architectural tradition and into current problems of urban design and city planning. In a town where every man's house is an enlarged bedroom of "non-committal space," the other interspersed spaces must serve as "family rooms" (parks), "parlors" (office-buildings), "entryways" (airports, harbors), and "guest dining rooms" (restaurants). Everything in Japanese life, he explains, has given the "bed-room house" and the "bed-town" a different significance from that of their apparent counterparts in the West. The Japanese city, like the Japanese house, must be judged from the inside out—not from its symmetry or neatness but from its ability to serve living people and to grow with them.

The Japanese city, of which Tokyo is his gargantuan example, is itself an organism—precisely because it has not been imprisoned in any architect's or planner's earlier dogma of how it would or must grow. He explains the apparent exception of Kyoto as due to a temporary Chinese influence. Amoeba-like, the Japanese townscape varies its shapes and assimilates to itself, creating a Hidden Order.

This book, brief though it is, can be a potent corrective, out of proportion to its size. It confronts the arrogant clairvoyance of Western city planners without becoming a brief for urban anarchy. Mr. Ashihara shows how, without anybody planning it, Japanese architecture has come to express the vitality of Japanese life. Here we discover the distinctive freedoms of an architecture unconfined by walls, unrooted in masonry foundations, committed not to the hard line or external symmetry, but to the fluidity of communities of living men and women. Here, too, we discover the special opportunities of the architecture of people eager to share the ever-present, changeful beauties of nature, and we are reminded of the limits of a Western architecture committed to form and facades.

Paradoxically, precisely by showing how different is the Japanese feeling for building from the Western and even from the Chinese, he helps us glimpse new possibilities for the Western house, the Western town, and the Western community. These could never be discovered by the perfunctory borrowing of architectural styles and structural features. And so Mr. Ashihara reminds us that a higher mission of the architect is not merely to fulfill his own cultural tradition, the peculiar opportunities of his place, but to enrich his works by understanding the arts first revealed to mankind in remote and unfamiliar places.

Daniel J. Boorstin
Washington, D.C.
October 1988

FOREWORD

Professor Ashihara and I first became acquainted in the 1960s and later were participants in Dr. Constantinos Doxiadis' conferences on human settlements. Since then we have met and visited frequently. As I have listened to Ashihara describe his many and varied projects in Japan, I have always treasured these moments with my friend, but to be able to read the manuscript of this book has provided me with a new perspective on our relationship.

My book *The Hidden Dimension*, published in 1966, was devoted to the subject of human perception and the use of space—the built environment as an extension of the human psyche. For years I had been a captive of this important and all-encompassing subject, but I found myself fighting an uphill battle when it came to making any significant impression on my American and European architectural colleagues, especially in persuading them that buildings were forms which both control and reflect human relationships. And what could be more important than human relationships?

In the United States and in Europe, as Ashihara makes clear, buildings perform primary functions which are directed toward the presentation of an appropriate facade (the architectural counterpart of the persona, masks worn by Greek actors symbolizing the public image).

The fascinating aspect of architecture is that it is congruent with culture, so that the entire building, down to the last detail, reflects the culture, as Ashihara points out. Japanese buildings are finished and properly built even in places the inhabitants cannot see, whereas the European and American model emphasizes only what can be seen from the front—the facade—and too often ignores the real needs of the inhabitants.

Ashihara's book is not only a statement of the hidden order in Japanese cities but is also by far the most coherent and truthful statement of the many cultural levels of contrast between East and West. I would place the book at the head of any list of required reading in schools of architecture in the United States as well as in Japan. For anyone who reads this book will see the architecture of both parts of the world in the matrix of culture and will in the process gain immeasurably in understanding the totality of the two cultures and why they may not always communicate to each other.

One last word: Professor Ashihara is a very modest man and, in spite of his many accomplishments, has expressed reservations concerning the need for such a book as this. It gives me great satisfaction to know that his unique and pioneering statement is now available for everyone to read.

Edward T. Hall
Santa Fe, New Mexico
September 1988

Chapter 1

A New Appraisal of the Tokyo Townscape

Why do the Japanese, even in modern Tokyo, take off their shoes before entering their homes? One may think this an insignificant, trivial question. Yet, it is, I believe, key to understanding the nature of the city of Tokyo. Its chaotic layout, fascinating if somehow inscrutable, is the result of an orientation to space quite different from that which governs the architecture, townscapes, and city planning of the West.

Until the Meiji period (1868–1912), architecture in Japan was almost exclusively post-and-beam, and in this tradition, it was the floor, rather than the wall, that became the focus of attention. The floor was elevated from the ground to enable under-floor ventilation—critical during the hot, humid summers. As people stepped up into the house, footwear was removed, and life unfolded on the floor level there. Walls, whether of fine palaces or ordinary dwellings, were relatively insignificant. They were not built to impress from the outside. The mild, temperate climate and luxuriant vegetation would, in any case, soon envelop any structure, obscuring its outlines. Inside, permanently installed dividing walls were minimal, with most of the space partitioned with sliding, removable panels. This gave the interior space a singularly fluid quality, and profoundly affected Japanese lifestyles and ways of thinking. This kind of space is noncommittal—not clearly bedroom or living room or dining room (it may be all three); perhaps it is living in such space that makes Japanese themselves inclined to be noncommittal in their behavior and ambiguous in their thinking.

What alerts one to this peculiarity in Japanese architecture is the contrast that may be found in Greek architecture, with its tradition of stone architecture. The Aegean climate is hot and dry; vegetation is scarce. A building, therefore, stands out distinctly in the landscape, a study in the play of light and shadow. In terms of aesthetics and design, this kind of environment must have been ideal for the development of the characteristics that distinguish Aegean stone architecture, among them symmetry, frontality, and symbolism.

Each time I encounter the architecture and the cities of the people in different regions of the world, I am reminded how people's ideas about architecture and the city are in many ways dictated by the climate and culture of their country. Of course, culture is what makes architecture and cities distinctive to begin with. As such, the Japanese style of dwelling stands alone, a world apart from the dwellings of Western cultures.

The first point of divergence is the climatic factor— the relationship of architecture to local temperature and, particularly, humidity. Climates around the world are of three main types: those that have hot, humid summers and cold, dry winters; those that have hot, dry summers and cold, humid winters; and those that are hot and humid all year round. The Japanese climate is of the first type, the climate of southern Europe falls under the second type, and that of Southeast Asia is an example of the third.

For a climate with hot, humid summers, buildings of wood are to be preferred. A deep roof, supported by posts, can leave the interior open to the out-of-doors, allowing for good ventilation. This, as I have said, is mainstream in Japanese architecture. Because walls do not play a significant structural role in this construction, their presence is of diminished importance. Instead, the floor and the roof are the crucial elements, thus affording an uninterrupted continuity between interior and exterior.

In southern Europe or the desert regions of the Middle East, by contrast, the summers are without rainfall and very dry. With scant vegetation, timber is not an economical building material. Masonry is the structure of choice, its thick, heavy, well-insulating walls providing protection against heat and dryness as well as cold and moisture. In the southern part of Spain, for example, the summers are very hot and humidity very low. If you open up the window and turn on a fan, the inside only gets hotter.

Japan has hot and humid summers as do the Southeast Asian countries, but unlike them it has cold, comparatively dry winters. This is probably one of the reasons why the country adapted so easily to certain Western ways.

People wonder how the Japanese have managed to survive the cold winters, living as they do in poorly insulated post-and-beam structure houses. In the South Pacific, temperature and humidity are roughly the same in both summer and winter, but in Japan (with the exception of the snowy regions on the northwestern side of the island of Honshu), the winters are generally dry and cold. The traditional Japanese house does not retain heat and has a relatively small proportion of solid wall area, but people manage to keep warm by other means. They dress in thick, padded clothing and adopt eating habits that promote warmth—stew-like dishes, hot tea, and of course, warmed *sake*. At night they take baths so hot as to be practically scalding before slipping into thick quilts that preserve body warmth. In other words, instead of attempting to warm up the space around them, each individual absorbs and maintains his own body warmth as much as possible.

Because of the open, uninsulable nature of wooden post-and-beam construction, the notion of heating the entire interior of a house was slow to develop. Where masonry construction retained heat, so that once the stone walls of a masonry building had been heated through, the house remained warm for some time, heating a Japanese house was considered as hopeless a task as heating the out-of-doors. In a country where stone and brick buildings hardly existed until the middle of the nineteenth century, central heating was unheard of. The notion of sitting in a thoroughly heated room in the depths of winter with a cold beer in hand was unimaginable.

And so climate has exerted a decisive impact on the way people live in various parts of the world. Even today climate has a decisive influence on the character of Japanese architecture, though with recent advances in building technology, there are fewer and fewer dwellings built in the Japanese post-and-beam style using uninsulated hanging walls. What wood construction structures we do see are more often than not built with Western-style stud walls and small windows. Instead of dwellings built to catch the breezes—the archetype loved by the Japanese of old—we are finding more that are constructed to shut out the breezes and are cooled instead with air conditioners. They are also well insulated against the cold of winter and equipped with central heating.

While recent architecture in Japan is essentially little different from that in Western countries, when it comes to private dwellings, the "shoes-off" lifestyle that has prevailed for centuries continues. No matter how the trappings of Japanese lives might change, there remains the unconscious feeling that the interior of the home is of a higher spatial order than the exterior, as demonstrated by the unwavering belief that the house is a clean place where one should not tread with footwear exposed to the dirt of the street.

This is one of the unspoken rules that govern the Japanese thinking and way of life, and it is basic to a lifestyle that can aptly be called floor-oriented. The customs and habits that have evolved from this simple act of taking shoes off indoors extend beyond the home to a generalized lifestyle and, in turn, have given birth to the unique townscapes and configurations of the Japanese city—in particular, Tokyo.

Just as climate differs from one region of the world to another, so the architecture and the nature of cities differ from country to country. A people has no choice but to build buildings and develop cities by methods that suit their climate and their traditions. This is not to say that one need be satisfied with the architecture, townscapes, or cities as they are today, but some appreciation for the hidden order that governs the seeming chaos of Japan's cities is essential before proceeding further.

The townscape of any country—and Tokyo represents the most dynamic example in Japan—was created by the people who settled there in the long course of history, evolving through time, through the interaction of the inhabitants and their environment. Because of this legacy of history, of course, it is impossible to redesign a disorderly city like Tokyo into a Paris or vice versa. One would be much wiser to assess Tokyo for what it is, recognizing its overall merits and seeking a firm understanding of its urban context. Then one might try to repair that which does not suit the demands of the current age and to preserve that which should not be lost.

One way to view Tokyo, then, is in terms of Gestalt. As F.G. Winter, the German philosopher and scholar of architecture, noted in a lecture in Japan, Gestalt psychology tends to approach things by visual measurement, by fluid, impermanent forms known as *Gestalten*. It is, he suggested, a concept not far removed from the Buddhist idea of the transcience of all things. The principle of the constant change of Gestalt on the axis of time is tantamount to the law of nature. Such is the city of Tokyo. It has a recognizable shape, but it is constantly changing. Like the flame of a candle, it appears to be unchanging, but what was there at one moment is not the same as an hour later.

Along this general line of thought, Benoit Mandelbrot's *Fractal Geometry of Nature* adds new insight. While Mandelbrot uncovered a random mathematical structure that lies behind beauty, he also discovered that the seeming chaos of nature embraces a flexible, orderly structure. This order evolved from random figures and, it occurred to me, explains quite neatly the idea of a "hidden order" that I have long believed to be inherent in the character of Japanese cities and Japanese architecture. Moreover, it is a hidden order that points to much of the perceived differences between Japanese culture and Western civilization. These differences are fundamental, and when they meet they often clash. I attempt here to probe behind certain cultural frictions, for I believe they can be traced to deeply entrenched cultural, even architectural, patterns. The ideas I address in this book—ways of designing space, the nature of order, use of space in human relations—are part of this effort.

Chapter 2

The View Within

Life on the Floor

The ceiling, the wall, and the floor represent the three elements of architecture. How these relate to interior architectural space in Japan as opposed to in the West is key to understanding the Japanese lifestyle—no less now in modern Tokyo than in more traditional times.

A first point of comparison is ceiling height. Ceilings in Japan are strikingly low by Western standards, and this applies not only to private residences, but to all kinds of architecture from hotels and restaurants to office buildings. It is true that Japanese are an average of ten centimeters shorter in stature than people of most Western countries,[1] and no doubt the lowness of ceilings may reflect that fact. The real reasons, however, can be traced, as I have said, to basic cultural and climatic factors.

In Japan's traditional post-and-beam wooden architecture, the floor is built off the ground, elevated as much as one meter to protect against the moisture that collects in the earth beneath it and to allow for better ventilation. Floors are made of long, smoothly polished wooden planks, often fitted with thick, cushiony *tatami* mats. Furnishings, such as beds, chairs, and tables, which are designed to lift human activity off of cold, damp floors in direct contact with the earth, are not necessary. All that is needed for sleeping or sitting is mattresses and cushions.

As a result of this type of orientation, daily activity inside the home unfolds largely on the level of the floor. Cooking and food preparation were done, and often still are, in an unelevated part of the house—in olden times in an earthen floored area—but for eating, sleeping, sitting, and all other activity, a person is never far off the floor. This means that the average line of vision—in modern homes and apartments as well— is at least 30 centimeters lower than it would be in a room that used tables, chairs, and beds. The cushions and thin mattresses spread directly on the *tatami* to accommodate sitting and sleeping needs are easy to clear away and store out of sight.

The amount of vertical space needed for human comfort, therefore, is less than when using tables and chairs. The low profile of traditional furnishings naturally contributes to the lower dimensions of interior space in the Japanese home, and the elevated structure of the dwelling, which overlooked its surroundings, adds to the downward-oriented line of vision of those within.

In the traditional Japanese house, door height is approximately 1.7 meters (5 *shaku*, 7 *sun*), and this is very low by international standards. At the smallest extreme are the 60-centimeter high entrances of tea ceremony houses through which one crouches to pass (fig. 1). Such architectural features are the result, of

Fig. 1. Low entrance to a tea ceremony hut (height, 60 centimeters), Sa-an, Gyokurin-in, Daitokuji, Kyoto.

course, of the complex of manners and customs that
evolved from a way of life carried out with posture and
line of vision generally turned downward.

Manners and customs have evolved to suit the floor-
oriented lifestyle. When entering a room, for example,
it is considered impolite to open the sliding door or
enter the room in a standing position. The most refined way to enter is to kneel, slide the door slightly
open with one hand, and then push it gently aside with
the other in a graceful movement, the body held in a
slight bow all the while, and to bow further from the
kneeling position before entering (figs. 2, 3). The line
of vision determined by this kind of etiquette is
oriented downward or straight outward (from the sitting position); it is rarely turned upward as it might be
in the high-ceilinged homes or marble palaces or
cathedrals of the West.

In the Japanese tradition, a dwelling was generally
considered somewhat temporary. Life itself, Buddhism
teaches, is transitory; moreover, the climate was
generally hospitable, and daily activity was largely
carried on out-of-doors. The ideal abode was un-
prepossessing, humble, and well harmonized with its
natural setting; massive or high structures were
eschewed. In the architecture of the Heian period, interiors were sometimes decorated with brightly colored
paintings but the posts and beams were unpainted,
natural wood, and architectural expression was basi-
cally simple and plain. In later tea ceremony architecture and the *sukiya* style, ceilings of natural materials

Fig. 2. How to open (*left, center*) and close (*right*) the sliding door to a traditional Japanese room.

Fig. 3. Bowing from a kneeling position on the *tatami*.

Fig. 4. Woven bullrush ceiling (*gama tenjō*).

were preferred, and styles that highlighted the texture of natural materials such as the *gama tenjo*, or woven bullrush ceiling, were especially favored (fig. 4). In the *saobuchi* ceilings of the early modern period (fig. 5), which were made of suspended ceiling boards supported by slender square rods visible from below, the

Fig. 5. Suspended ceiling (*saobuchi tenjō*).

features of greatest refinement were mainly the fine grain and width of the wood used, for they were usually unpainted and plain. Some wall apertures were made by simply exposing the wall framework (fig. 6).

In the West, the ceilings of most prominent buildings, from stone cathedrals to Renaissance villas, are extremely high; often they are richly decorated with colorful frescoes. The domes of Islamic mosques are adorned with tile mosaics well known for their lavishness and color.

With the exception of structures built under the direct influence of China, such as the Buddhist temples of the Asuka and Nara period, the Amida-dō of the Byōdō-in, and the large halls of the Nijō Palace built in the Momoyama period (1568–1603), however, high ceilings and colored wall paintings were never popular in Japan, and no examples can be found in architecture built from the beginning of the early modern period (roughly 1600–1867).

Some years ago, while in Italy, I toured the Villa Rotonda, a stately residence located on a hill in the suburbs of Vicenza. This famous example of the Palladian style has influenced architects around the world. It has porticoes on all four sides, each supported by six Ionian orders, and presents a majestic symmetry and frontality from whatever direction one approaches. I later had occasion to visit another villa designed by Palladio, the Villa Foscari in the Venetian suburb of Malcontenta. Invited to an evening banquet, I had a leisurely opportunity to absorb the feeling of the

Fig. 6. Window created by exposing the framework of the wall (*shitaji mado*).

building. Like the Villa Rotonda, it has a symmetrical portico at the top of the front steps, a row of Ionian columns, and an extremely high dome inside under the cross-style roof, decorated with magnificent frescoes.

Although it is not the kind of architectural space that inspires or appeals to Japanese, I could readily see why this building is considered a great work of art in the history of architecture. Japanese are accustomed to spaces that direct the line of vision downward, so these high ceilings would simply inspire awe. We understand them in religious structures, but are not likely to adopt them for residential buildings. How must it feel to live daily in spaces of such immense proportions? Am I the only one who feels so small and miserably insignificant inside those vast and echoing rooms?

The Japanese architectural tradition is well expressed in the jottings of a priest of the medieval period named Yoshida Kenkō (1283–1350):

There is a charm about a neat and proper dwelling house, although this world, 'tis true, is but a temporary abode. Even the moonshine, when it strikes into the house where a good man lives in peaceful ease, seems to gain in friendly brilliancy.

The man is to be envied who lives in a house, not of the modern, garish kind, but set among venerable trees, with a garden where plants grow wild and yet seem to have been disposed with care, verandas and fences tastefully arranged, and all its furnishings simple but antique. . . .

A house should be built with the summer in view. In winter one can live anywhere, but a poor dwelling in summer is unbearable. Deep water does not give a cool sensation. Far cooler is a shallow running stream. A room with sliding doors is lighter than one with doors on hinges. When the ceiling is high the room is cold in winter and difficult to light. As for construction, people agree in admiring a place with plenty of spare room as being pleasing to the eye and at the same time useful for all sorts of purposes.[2]

To this quite old account of the Japanese preference for low ceilings, let me add the observations of architectural historian Hirotarō Ōta, regarding the ceiling in traditional architecture. Ōta writes that because the eaves of buildings were long and activity was carried out at a low level (that is, on the floor) the parts of space that needed to be lighted were markedly different from those of Western residential architecture. The space is brightest relatively close to the floor, and grows darker as it nears the ceiling. The use of color in interiors, he says, follows the same principle, contrasting with that of Western-style residences, where bright colors are often used in the upper parts of rooms.[3] The ideal ceiling was deliberately made low and dark so as to be practically unnoticeable. This, in fact, bears out my belief that the floor is the governing element of Japanese post-and-beam architecture.

In the United States, ceiling height is sometimes an indication of rank or social status. The usual height for offices is 2.70 meters but may be raised to 3 meters for the quarters of high-ranking executives. Executives generally have small individual rooms with a D/H ratio (distance between walls to wall height) far smaller than that of the main office, often approaching the D/H ratio of religious architecture. Ceiling height in Japanese offices is 2.40–2.70 meters at the highest, and I have never heard a company director complain that he does not feel as if his status has changed because the ceiling of his office is too low. In the United States, however, architects are often told that it is normal practice to make the ceilings of executive rooms as high as possible.

The height of doorways in Japanese-style architecture is determined by the inside dimensions of the frieze rail (*nageshi*) at between 1.70 and 1.74 meters, traditionally favoring fairly modest proportions. In the United States or Europe, such a height would not be practical, for people's average height is greater than that of Japanese. Proportionately speaking, too, it would appear ill-fitting and cheap. Doorways in modern Western architecture are as a rule quite high, sometimes reaching all the way to the ceiling. When Westerners come to Japan, many are surprised to encounter the low doorways standard in all public facilities, from trains to meeting rooms, and I have seen many an unsuspecting visitor crack his head on a lintel.

In considering the qualities of Japan's architecture of the floor, I believe it is helpful to reappraise carefully the nature of such architectural elements as the ceiling and the wall. It is the different character of these elements that shows us the distinctions between the traditional wooden architecture of Japan and the masonry architecture of the West.

In Praise of Shadows

I have long been fascinated by the Gestalt relationship between figure and ground, such as illustrated in the reversal-effect illustrated by Edgar Rubin's vase-faces (fig. 7). In *The Aesthetic Townscape* I discussed the application of this idea to various kinds of architectural and urban space.[4] When I described this approach to the appreciation of space to audiences in Chinese universities, there was inordinate interest, no doubt because the principle of figure-ground reversal is akin to the ancient Chinese theory of *yin* and *yang*.

According to Chinese thought, the essence of all things is *qi*, which alternatively takes the form of *yin* and of *yang*; when *yang* reaches its culmination, it gives way to *yin*; when *yin* reaches its culmination, it gives way to *yang*. The cosmic harmony produced by the spontaneous transformation of one into the other is basic to Far Eastern mysticism and a world apart from Cartesian dualism.

Now, in my summer travels in Europe, particularly in Italy, Spain, and among the islands of the Aegean sea, I am keenly aware of the absolute contrast be-

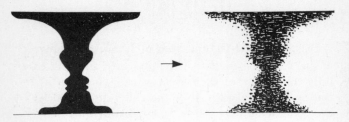

Fig. 7. Edgar Rubin vases.

tween sunlight and shadow. The air is dry, the sun is strong, and everything is cast in either bright sunshine or shade; there is no fuzzy zone in which the two intermingle. As Marcel Breuer observed, the spectator's seats in the Spanish bullring are either in the shade or out in the blazing sun[5] (fig. 8). Light and shade seem pitted against one another, and the contours of a sculpture under the bright Grecian sun are thrown into striking contrast. I have mused that the sunny climate of the region around the Aegean Sea must have had considerable influence on the evolution of Western dualistic thinking and the clear distinctions between black and white, good and evil, sun and shadow.

Since the end of the Vietnam war, a sense of deadlock has begun to pervade Western civilization, and many have sought to go beyond the dualism that has dominated European and American thinking for centuries. Fritjof Capra, author of *The Tao of Physics*, explains the cultural crisis aptly: The imbalance between *yin* and *yang* in individual values—"the consistent preference for *yang* values"—is the root of the malaise of European and North American civilization. Strong is always more highly valued than weak, action

Fig. 8. Contrast of light and shadow in a Spanish bullring (*sol y sombra*).

more than quiet, rational thought more than intuited wisdom, science more than religion, and competition more than harmony. This one-sided development has reached a critical stage, bringing Western man face to face with a dangerous social, environmental, ethical, and spiritual situation. At the same time, he writes, the signs of an amazing trend are appearing—just as the ancient Chinese say, when *yang* reaches its culmination, it gives way to *yin*. What is happening, according to Capra, is an attempt to regain the balance between the *yin* and *yang* dimensions of humanity through the destruction of the domination of the masculine and the rational in human endeavor and values.[6]

If one considers the problem of form and content in architecture in terms of Capra's ideas, perhaps the cultural malaise of Europe and America may be seen to stem from the fact that the active, the rational, the scientific, and the competitive have been given too much emphasis. The presence of light, in other words, was too strong, like the unmerciful Grecian sun. There was no room for shadow, and no intermediate, fuzzy buffer zone between them. In architectural terms, the surface form of a building can be described as a manifestation of light, while its content, the interior concealed behind its outer facade, can be described as shadow.

Traditional Japanese architecture is characterized by large roofs and long eaves, a kind of structure that provides ample shade against the hot summer sun. The novelist Jun'ichirō Tanizaki (1886–1965), a connoisseur of the beauties of shade and shadow, writes in an essay on the subject:

> In the course of time our ancestors, living in dwellings that were inevitably dark, learned to see the beauties to be found in the shades of shadows, and to cultivate the shade for their aesthetic pleasure. The beauty of a Japanese interior, indeed, is above all the result of the shades of light and dark. Westerners are surprised at the utter simplicity of Japan's *tatami*-floored rooms, and it is understandable that they must feel somewhat depressed by the unremitting gray of the walls and complete lack of decoration. Their lack of appreciation for such interiors derives from the fact that they have not grasped the mystique of shadows.[7]

Indeed, there was a day when people enjoyed the dim light cast by candles or paper-covered lanterns and when the interplay of light and dark was better appreciated. Today, thanks to affluence and advances in science and technology—the light dimension—the shadow aspects that are part and parcel of humanity have been put aside and all but forgotten. What a contrast there is between the marble sculptures of Greece, bathed in the strong sunlight of their exterior settings, and the Buddhist sculptures of Japan, shut away in the dusky interiors of temples (fig. 9). Or between the heroic columns that support the facades of Greek temples and the unassuming bracket complexes of the

Fig. 9. Image inside a Buddhist temple.

wayō, *karayō*, or *tenjikuyō* styles that lie half hidden under the eaves of ancient Japanese temples.

With the growth of industrialized society, populations rapidly began to concentrate in the cities, and the urban environment became artificial and alienating. In the whirl of energy generated by human activity in such an environment, life appears superficially—at least in the material sense—to be satisfying, but spiritually, it is not in the least fulfilled. In the turbulent environment of the city it becomes harder and harder for people to establish close relationships with one another or to enjoy the beauties of nature and the shifting seasons. Again, we are reminded of Tanizaki's praises of shadow. The love of shadows that he says our ancestors developed has certainly faded in this day and age.

People once were capable not only of grasping the meaning of light, where things exist, but of recognizing the equivalent significance of shadow, where there is nothing. An example is the dry landscape garden at Ryōanji in Kyoto (fig. 10). In a rectangular space, fifteen rocks are arranged in groups in a sea of gray pebbles. When observed from a dualistic viewpoint, one might quickly see the distinction between the rocks and the pebbles that fill the surrounding space, but hardly contemplate the relationship between the two. The garden takes on a whole new meaning, however, if one recognizes the potential existence of the portion occupied by the pebbles alone.

Suppose, for example, the garden was based on a

Fig. 10. Dry landscape at Ryōanji, Kyoto.

massive rock foundation with portions protruding only at those fifteen spots; that would be enough to validate the existence of the portion not occupied by the rocks. As it happens, the contours of the rocks appear this way, but if there were some movement of the earth's crust, it might change. The outline of the rocks does exist, but it is not a matter of symmetry or vertical volume; they are naturally shaped rocks, and although they are scattered in seeming isolation from one another, there is a kind of continuity in their arrangement.

This might be understood in terms of how the tigress moves her three cubs across a river. If she leaves her fierce first-born cub with any of the other cubs, he might tear it to pieces, so she first takes him to the opposite side of the river and leaves him alone while she returns for another cub and re-crosses the river. She then carries the eldest back to the other side, leaves him, again alone, while transporting the third cub, and finally returns for her fractious offspring. To discover such a continuity where none is apparent and to savor the beauties of delicate shadows is to come upon what we may call the "hidden order." Again, this stands in sharp contrast to the clarity, symmetry, and perfection that are the ideals of Western architecture from ancient Greece through the Renaissance.

Inherent in the *yang/yin* dynamic is the evolution of the masculine into the feminine and vice versa. The survival of a city or of individual buildings within it, I believe, requires a shift from "form" to "content" and from "the whole" to "the parts." This contrast is evident in the comparison of Paris and Tokyo. Paris is a city divided with foresight into parts "cut" from the whole, while Tokyo follows the sense of the whole enveloping all its various parts. Paris is a splendid, beautiful city, indeed, but may be encountering difficulty when it comes to adjusting to the needs of the twenty-first century. Its masonry architecture makes it, in a way, a static and inorganic monument of the past. Tokyo, however, remains a synchronic whole, tenaciously surviving by rather an amoebic adaptability. It is an ugly, chaotic metropolis, but it is organic and constantly in the throes of change. I cannot help wishing at times that the amoeba would replicate its parts with somewhat more care, but its vigor is not to be denied.

The Changing "Bed Town"

Since ancient times, Japanese have lived in post-and-beam wood construction dwellings. As I have described, they were elevated off the ground in order to protect against the dampness of the earth and to allow for sufficient ventilation. In China, too, wood was the main structural material of architecture, but there are regions of dry climate where buildings of sun-dried brick (*zhuān*) predominate. In most of the ordinary houses, the floors are firmly packed, dried earth. The basic structure rests on four posts, and beds equipped with mosquito nets are used for sleeping. Getting into one of these beds at night would seem rather like entering a private bedroom. To a visitor, such as I was, the Chinese do not hesitate to show their whole houses, bedrooms and all, and this is perhaps because it is customary, as in the West, to enter the house with one's shoes on.

Let me explain what I mean. The Japanese house, governed as it is by the architecture of the floor, is entered only after taking off one's outdoor footwear. Dust and dirt from the outside are thus left in the entryway, and the floors, be they wood planks, *tatami*, linoleum, or carpet, are kept relatively clean. You may shed your coat here and drop your bags there—right on the floor—and even sprawl full length for a rest if you wish. Tables and chairs, beds and coatracks are hardly necessary, for the floors are clean enough to sit on or lay things on directly. It is quite easy for this kind of space to become cluttered with things, however, as there tends to be little room available in the built-in cupboards and closets. The whole house, in fact, where one pads around in his stocking feet or slippers, is like a bedroom.

Historian Shōzaburō Kimura writes that "in contrast to the homes of Westerners, in which space is treated as on the same level as the out-of-doors, and where shoes are worn, in a Japanese house, one takes off his shoes upon entering. This allows the dweller to act with a sense of ease and relaxation that the Western-style house permits only in the bedroom. Not only visitors to Japan, but Japanese who have lived abroad for some time remark that these houses of elevated structure and *tatami*-matted floors seem much like large beds.''[8]

Imagine, thus, that each house in Japan is a private bedroom. The city becomes a mammoth cluster of ''bedrooms'' interspersed with ''family rooms'' (parks), ''parlors'' (office buildings), ''entryways'' (airports, harbors), and the like. You may think such an analogy is completely off the wall, so to speak, but it does offer some insight into the nature of Japanese society and its cities.

Tokyo and other major cities in Japan are surrounded by suburbs from which people commute to jobs and schools located in downtown areas. These suburbs are located so far away—perhaps an hour or two away by train, subway, and bus—that working people employed in the center of the cities do little more than sleep in their homes. This may be why the suburbs are known in Japanese as ''bed towns.'' For reasons of time and distance, there are relatively few hours of relaxation to be spent at home and little opportunity to invite friends or relatives over to visit, as is common in the West. The breadwinner of the household, usually the husband, leaves early in the morning and returns late at night, except on Sundays, with statistics showing that most working people spend their holidays quietly, watching TV, in a home that functions as a box-like bedroom. No wonder it is so difficult to realize city planners' visions of a new style of ''community.''

As long as Japanese live like this—each in his small, isolated bedroom—we will hardly be convinced that our country is the advanced economic superpower we are told it is. Of course, our homes are filled with the latest electric appliances and fashionable interiors, but these conveniences give us no sense of fulfillment culturally. Unlike Western homes, which often have paintings on the walls, perhaps a sculpture in the front hall, and a study filled with books, Japanese dwellings have not the space for such luxuries. What space there is is more likely to be taken up by more essential household fixtures or furniture.

In the traditional home there was invariably a *tokonoma*, or recessed alcove, built into the main room of the house where a painting or scroll reflecting the season of the year, a vase of flowers, or a treasured art object might be displayed (fig. 11). In the rapidly moving tide of urbanization, however, often even this modest corner dedicated to contemplative or artistic beauty has vanished.

Although Japan may be an economic superpower—the largest creditor nation in the world—the space in which individual people live remains cramped and unattractive, and lifestyles lack much in the way of cultural and artistic fulfillment. Insofar as Japanese live in bedroom-like dwellings, the kind of human interaction that goes on in the living rooms of people in other countries is not to be had. Instead, friends and relatives are met in public places. The entertainment and restaurant business in Japan serves needs well, and amusement spots, urban and rural, are always filled with people. Visitors often voice their amazement at

Fig. 11. Alcove for displaying works of art (*tokonoma*).

these vortexes of human energy, but it is well that they be perceived in context.

Nevertheless, changes are occurring in the "bed town." Japanese are quite attached to the old-style post-and-beam dwelling through which the summer breezes waft and on whose *tatami* floors we are wont to sprawl with a good book. If we must put up with cramped and shabby quarters, we comfort ourselves with a postage-stamp garden off the back veranda, a bamboo blind to ward off the hot summer sun (and the neighbors' curious stares), and a cage with a captured insect whose bell-like sound transports us to the countryside—hours away by any form of transportation. But these comfortable abodes are vulnerable to fires and burglars and cannot be left for long without someone to look after them. Housewives are imbued with the habit of worrying if there is no one watching the house for more than two or three hours.

In this day and age, however, Japanese women are not always happy with being relegated to the role of housekeeper and guardian of the hearth. They have had enough of being chained to the house and the "bedroom" suburb. Women are claiming the right to be treated equally with men for the opportunity to work outside the home.

It is well to keep in mind, I believe, that equal rights for men and women and the problems of urban development and housing are very closely related—in fact, we might say they are two sides of the same coin. If both men and women are to be free to go out and work, it is crucial that we find solutions to the problems of long-distance commuting and fragile, "bedroom" suburb homes. Houses that will not go up in flames at the drop of a match and that can be securely locked are urgently needed. These priorities are already beginning to have an effect on new housing in our cities, it is true, but remain luxuries as yet available only to a few. A genuine change in the role of women will not come about until a way is found to close the gap between those women who have access to conditions that liberate them from the home and those who do not.

Japanese may wonder if there is any possible solution to the dilemma of cities such as Tokyo, which overflow with people in the daytime and echo with emptiness at night, and of the "bedroom" suburbs, so far away from places of work. The simplistic solution might be to redevelop city centers, building scores of high-rise condominiums in inner-city areas from which people can commute quickly to their jobs, carrying the keys to their apartments in their pockets. I doubt, however, that this idea could gain much enduring appeal. After all, the ideal of a house with a garden, no matter how tiny it may be, that imparts a feeling of communion with nature is deeply entrenched among Japanese, and is not likely to fade despite the realities of overpopulation.

If this is so, the only feasible way to get around the problem is to find ways to distribute the population more evenly among smaller local cities so that people can live in areas where a good-sized plot of land upon which to build a home is readily available. Decentralization, of course, means fostering local culture in various parts of the country and dispersing industry in order to draw people away from the huge megalopolises. Whether or not we can achieve a better distribution of population, in fact, may determine the future of this country. The key to better cities in the twenty-first century, I believe, is in rediscovering the identity of our local cities.

Chapter 3

The Hidden Order

The Ambiguity of Outline

How would you define the outline of an object? Is it a distinct form like the Gestalt shapes created by the borderline between the black and white spaces of figure and ground? Or is it more amorphous, like the outline of a human body? The outline of a human figure may at first seem clear and distinct, but when you think about it, that outline is a constantly changing shape—you slough off layers of skin every time you take a bath, cut your fingernails, adopt a new hairstyle, or shave. Certainly our body outline changes subtly all the time (fig. 12).

Likewise, we can consider the line that divides the land and the sea. Take, for example, the distance between point A and point B—say between Aomori and Tokyo (fig. 13). If we calculate the distance on an ordinary road map, we arrive at a rough estimate of the length of the coastline, about 3,000 kilometers. Now we obtain a topographical map that shows the area in greater detail; with the coastline more accurately depicted than before, we can see that it is actually much longer than we thought.[9]

In *The Fractal Geometry of Nature*, Benoit B. Mandelbrot says, "There are various ways of evaluating length . . . coastline length turns out to be an elusive notion that slips between the fingers of one who wants to grasp it. All measurement methods lead to the conclusion that the typical coastline's length is very large and so ill-determined that it is best considered infinite."[10] The shape of a coastline changes constantly with shifting tides. If the coast were composed of vertical, rocky cliffs, the tides would not greatly alter the configuration of the coastline, but a shore of sandy beaches will be reshaped by the tides with each advancing hour. My point is this: the borderline between even such totally different and existentially opposite things as land and sea is not as clear and distinct as one might at first think.

If we take the land as the Gestalt figure, and the sea as the ground, then the outline between figure and ground clearly belongs to the land. However, the sea is not bottomless—beneath it lies the land, and the coastline just happens to be determined by the sea level at a particular time—the actual outline flows in and out all the time (fig. 14). In other words, once you recognize the hidden Gestalt order of the sea's outline and gaze again at the sea as you would at Edgar Rubin's vase-faces, you see a very different outline. Moreover, this borderline is the embodiment of the perpetual transformation of *yin* into its opposite, *yang*, and *yang* into *yin*. There is a constant appearing and disappearing, enlargening and shrinking, that occurs in the time sequence. The changing shapes are the result of recognizing the potential for latent shapes

Fig. 12. What is the exact outline of the human body?

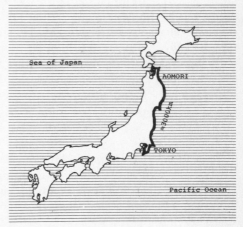

Fig. 13. Map of Japan showing coastline between Aomori and Tokyo.

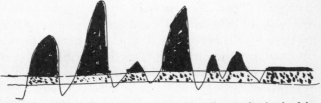

Fig. 14. The shape of the land changes depending on the depth of the water.

where there is no apparent shape.

A coastline, therefore, is not a clear-cut outline as is the borderline between figure and ground in a Gestalt figure. We are forced to acknowledge that the existence of an intermediary territory incessantly changes, both physically and conceptually, causing intrusions into both inner and outer space in accordance with such phenomena as the rising and falling of the tides. Western dualistic thought, beginning with the Greek philosophers, is traditionally reluctant to deal with this intermediate territory. Other traditions, on the other hand, attach considerable importance to this realm, as does Japan's, with its affinity for ambiguity and incompleteness. Japanese ideas on ambiguity are also related to the concepts of the new-age sciences of Fritjof Capra.

The differing views regarding the definition of an outline are important when considering form in architecture, the aesthetics of the townscape, and the appearance of cities. The Western-type treatment of space and design (and I would include China's here) in architecture and urban planning is apt to be centripetal, beginning with the whole and then proceeding to its parts. The outline between a building and its surroundings or between a city and the country around it has traditionally been quite distinct. We can see this in the frontal, symmetrical lines of the Parthenon. It is also true of the ancient Chinese city Xian and the medieval castletowns of Italy, in which the outline of the city, formed by the ramparts that surround it, produced a clear shape from the beginning.

In contrast to this is the centrifugal character of buildings or cities that start with individual parts and expand, the proliferation of parts defining the shape in a random manner. Examples include the traditional architecture and typical townscapes of Japan, which are asymmetrical to begin with and where it is not at all unusual to expand spontaneously in any direction. The huge megalopolis of Tokyo and, similarly, other large Japanese cities illustrate this best: their endless sprawl encroaches on the surrounding countryside like a silkworm munching at a mulberry leaf. As a whole, the shape of these cities is extremely unstable and undefined, for their fringes are surrounded by an intermediary, ambiguous zone that is in constant flux.

Close observation of urban environments in Japan reveals that there is some wisdom in allowing for such undefined outlines. If an outline must be clearly delineated, it is necessary to impose restraints on the function of architecture or on the lifestyles within the area. Building codes are established, and town planning or zoning ordinances are enacted. It becomes necessary to place constraints on individual freedoms. Building and urban planning policy in Japan is considerably looser and more ambiguous than that in European countries, and this is the result of the strong resistance Japanese have to giving up freedom of movement for the sake of regularity of forms or clarity of outlines.

Along the Romantic Highway in southern Germany, for example, are beautiful towns such as Rothenburg, enclosed by medieval ramparts. The houses within the city walls are distinctive, but all have gabled roofs and all conform to regulations set down by these communities with regard to the color of walls and other architectural details. Even in the city of Paris, there is little freedom to diverge from established forms and styles. Emphasis is placed on preserving the outline of buildings, and great effort is made to do away with elements that might disturb the outline, such as utility poles, cables, exterior advertisements, hanging signs, and the like.

This outline, in fact, can be said to determine the appearance of the city in the West. Its form is an integrated whole, and there is not much leeway for change once completed. There is also little impetus to break up or destroy that whole. This concern with and emphasis upon form is what I call "architecture of the wall." Japanese architecture, on the other hand, the "architecture of the floor," gives priority to content. Content evolves in response to societal change, but form, once determined, is pretty hard to alter.

The practice of setting standards for the height or configuration of buildings, as often observed in Paris and other cities, was never very popular in Japan, with rare exceptions. On the contrary, there was complete freedom regarding the shape or location of windows and other features closely related to building outline, as well as for the materials of color of the walls. This lack of unity is, in addition, made to seem more chaotic by the inclusion of projecting signboards, rooftop advertising towers, hanging banners, and electric

poles, amid various trees and shrubs, gates, and concrete walls. Bedding is draped over balcony railings
and wash is hung under eaves, creating even further
convolutions in the outlines of architecture. (If the
movement to make cities more green continues, the
outline of architecture will grow even more blurred, until it becomes practically undetectable. Perhaps the
dryness of the summers in southern Europe, where
there is less vegetation, is related to the greater tendency for clarity of architectural outlines.)

What are the implications of either clarity or ambiguity of outline in architecture? Where the outline is
clear, a distinct form emerges that possesses a certain
artistic quality. Where the outline is unclear, form is
random or amorphous, like a spontaneous cluster of
organisms or the branching of a tree. If, as I suggest,
there is a "hidden order" in such amorphousness,
then it cannot be said to be complete chaos, and architecture and cities characterized by it have a potential not sufficiently appreciated until now.

The Amoeba City

Roland Barthes, after a visit to Tokyo, observed that
while the center of a European city may be a cathedral
or market where population and people converge, the
center of a Japanese city may not be that clear.[11] There
is a central area of Tokyo, for example—the moat-
encircled Imperial Palace—but it consists mostly of im-
maculately kept gardens inhabited by the royal family
and their staff. The surrounding city is crowded and

congested, with little that might give it form or focus. Its boundaries are ill-defined, sprawling wildly in every direction. It grows and flourishes in fits and starts without any kind of long-term urban planning. One section may be burned out by fire here, but a new section will spring up over there; one quarter may become run-down, but another will flourish next to it.

Tokyo is the perfect example of the fluid, regenerating city. It was levelled by fire many times during the Edo period, and a major part was burned to the ground in the Great Kanto Earthquake and Fire of 1923. Even after the devastating bombings of World War II, it did not become an abandoned ruin; it survived and revived with even greater vigor. Many of Europe's metropolises are plagued by the so-called doughnut phenomenon, or depopulation of the city core, but the heart of Tokyo—and most of Japan's cities—remains vital. This is the result of a healthy—if somewhat hyper—metabolism, making the city the scene of constant renewal and change. The cores of Western cities, with their indestructible masonry structures, on the other hand, suffer from stagnation and rigidity.

Tokyo, thus, is an "amoeba city" with its amorphous sprawl and the constant change it undergoes, like the pulsating body of the organism. And as with an amoeba, Tokyo demonstrates a physical integrity and the capacity for regeneration when damaged. Whether the amoeba city is good or bad, it does persevere.

Even the ferroconcrete buildings once thought to stand forever have turned out to be quite frail, their walls corroded by acid rain and other scourges of a contaminated environment. Many of the buildings being torn down in Tokyo today were built in the 1920s, having endured for only 50 or 60 years. Both structurally and functionally, the very infrastructure has turned out to have a relatively short life span.

Today, rapid changes in society are calling for new functions for cities and some modification of the nature of architecture. Faced with a building whose exterior tile is flaking off, whose metallic curtain walls have corroded, whose elevators or air conditioners no longer work well, or which does not have strong enough floors, high enough ceilings, or powerful enough electrical wiring to accommodate the introduction of high-tech communications and computer equipment, the Japanese would tend to decide that it is wisest to construct a new, more efficient building. Japanese are accustomed to thinking of architecture as temporary; the notion of this earthly world as being "but a transient abode" has a long tradition going back to early modern times. In fact, the changeless monuments of masonry architecture of the West, preserved and lived in for literally centuries, are somewhat curious monuments of the past.

The city halls facing the Piazza Signoria in Florence and overlooking the Piazza del Campo in Sienna have dominated their respective cities for several centuries since the Renaissance, and they continue to serve the same function they always have. City halls in Japan, on the other hand, are not looked upon by citizens as such important structures, and many of these edifices built soon after World War II are now being rebuilt or renovated. Even Tokyo's city hall, a prominent example of postwar architecture designed by Kenzō Tange, is soon to be demolished—because it is too small and too old to meet the needs of the present era—and a new high-rise building somehow resembling Notre Dame, also designed by Tange, constructed.

How does the amoeba city change over time? Japan has been rapidly modernized and industrialized in the four decades since the end of the last world war, and its population has concentrated in its large cities. Thirty million people live within a thirty-mile radius in Tokyo today. Unlike the long-term urban planning projects that have been undertaken in Western countries, city building in Japan has proceeded in a rather makeshift manner, changing course midway in accordance with immediate demands and new developments. There do exist such apparently long-term projects as the National Comprehensive Development Program, but even this is very short-term compared to similar projects in other countries and it has been subject to frequent change and revision. Although trial and error is not permissible when it comes to land development and urban planning, social change in Japan occurs very rapidly. Use of short-term development plans, amended and corrected whenever necessary, has often brought better results than rigid, long-term planning.

In most cases, for example, streets are built for functional purposes alone; little thought is given to aesthetic concerns. If the noise of traffic becomes unbearable to residents along the city expressways, unsightly sound-muffling walls are thrown up along their sides. To keep pedestrians from blocking busy intersections, spider-like elevated walkways are built. (Sometimes I think our street-planning authorities are more lacking in all aesthetic sensibility and awareness of the inherent cultural role of thoroughfares than any in the world.)

There was a time when roads and streets were colored and shaped by the local culture through which they passed. The old Tokaido highway that ran between the center of old Edo—Tokyo of today—and Kyoto was punctuated with 53 stations, each with its own distinctive flavor and atmosphere, and many of these places were immortalized in poetry and art. Before the proliferation of automobiles, too, the old Nikko highway and the mountain roads of Hakone were spots of scenic beauty, the roads lined with towering cedars that had stood for centuries. When main streets are built in today's large cities, it is important to incorporate an adequate buffer zone between the thoroughfare and the surrounding area. It is too late to do anything after the construction is completed and residents sue the city for destroying their environment. Street planning cannot be based solely on the priority of transportation between one point and another; it must incorporate an appreciation for the locales through which the streets will pass.

At present, the owner of a piece of land in Japan is

free to divide up his property in any way he likes. Often, people will do this because of high inheritance taxes, and even if a city tries to consolidate land, properties have become so irregular that standardizing plots is practically impossible. This is true of Tokyo as elsewhere in Japan. Since plots are of peculiar shape and size, the structures built are often oddly designed. One gets pencil-like buildings with space for little but stairways or elevators. Building sites are often so irregular that it is difficult to arrange structures in an orderly fashion, resulting in a townscape that is like a set of badly aligned teeth.

Even if one attempted to consolidate building sites through housing or redevelopment programs such as those adopted in some countries, the delicacy and complexity of adjusting the interests of landowners in Japan would often make the process impractical. Under the circumstances, there is little that can be accomplished by administrative measures for widening the roads, consolidating the land or attempting urban redevelopment. The best way seems to be for individual property owners to make the fullest use of their land within the legal limits. It is inevitable that a city built with this kind of short-range vision should appear disorderly and confusing.

Of the cities built in the nineteenth century, Paris is said to be the most beautiful. A masterful coordination has been achieved in eave and floor height and in the fenestrations of its masonry architecture, giving the streets an attractive harmony that is world famous.

And yet, in the commercial districts, which sustain the very life of the city, there is a severe shortage of office space. It is even said that the unemployment rate is increasing because the city refuses to permit the construction of modern commercial office buildings made of glass and metal lest they mar the townscape.

I imagine that Parisians look upon the intense energy and apparent confusion of cities in Japan like Tokyo with a mixture of contempt and envy. The coming twenty-first century will be an era of sophisticated information technology. It will be necessary to lay optical fiber and lines for the information network system beneath the streets in our cities and to channel them to every part of our buildings. Will a city like Paris, where fundamental architectural change is impossible, be able to adapt? Perhaps we will all be compelled to reevaluate the merits of the amoeba-like changefulness of a city like Tokyo.

It is certainly true that Tokyo is chaotic and lacking in artistic coordination as well as clear identity. Nevertheless, a tremendous urban population has managed to live in relative harmony, and has been responsible for achievements in economic development that have astonished the world. Cities in the West may give greater priority to form than does Tokyo, but with its concern for content Tokyo thrives according to an order hidden within its chaos. If there were no such order, how could the citizens of the world's second largest city lead the lives they do in such reasonable comfort?

Mandelbrot's notion of a flexible orderly structure embracing randomness in what is apparently chaos is critical here. At first glance, Tokyo looks chaotic (fig. 15). But if we consider that there is an invisible order, a random-switch mechanism through which each level of the whole structure tolerates some haphazardness so as to respond to changes in the environment—rather like the action of genes in the development of a multicellular organism—then we begin to see an order in the city structure.[12] The whole of Tokyo is a perpetual formation and re-formation of parts, which are endowed with a measure of randomness and haphazardness. Parts make up the whole of an individual structure, but that whole is a part in a higher level of the order. The city is an organic entity, which undergoes constant change and development, even to severing and discarding unnecessary parts.

If one subjected the symmetrical, frontal, face-oriented configurations of Paris to computer graphic processes used to input random order through figure development processes, the result would probably be a city like Tokyo. After all, both cities have the basic genes of a city. If any part of Tokyo embodies the whole, then Tokyo perhaps represents the concept of hidden order. By contrast, Western cities would fulfill the concept of explicit order.

To speak of the hidden order, not metaphysically but practically, in terms of the functions of the city, let us look at the subject of water supply and the sewer system, two vital utilities of city life. Japan is blessed with clean water in great abundance, and public water supply systems are exceedingly well developed throughout the country. We take clean water very much for granted, and tap water is drinkable everywhere. It is relatively uncommon around the world for the water used in flush toilets and the water you mix with your whiskey to come from the same source.

Sewer systems in Europe date back to the castle-towns of medieval times. Cities were encircled by high walls, and at sundown, the people and even their domesticated animals were gathered inside and the gates locked. The cities were paved with stone, and the buildings were uniformly of stone masonry construction. Obviously the disposal of human and animal wastes posed problems almost more serious than the defense of the city walls against enemy assaults. No doubt necessity played a large role in the development of sewer systems, as intolerable stench and the spread of infectious disease were constant concerns. Records tell how the city of Paris adopted a sewer system in order to combat epidemic diseases, how in London, after the devastating cholera epidemic of 1848, flush toilets became the standard.[13]

Unlike in Europe, where sewage was viewed only as a source of stench and disease and the building of sewer systems was advocated as a top priority, in Japan it was seen as an organic by-product, and much more emphasis was put on maintaining a pure water supply. Until modern times, streets and roads in

Fig. 15. View of the chaotic townscape of Tokyo.

Japan were rarely paved, but it did not make much difference in terms of public sanitation because footwear was traditionally removed before entering homes as well as workshops and business establishments. Here again, I am reminded of the great impact this shoes-off custom has had on the way of life in Japan.

As urbanization spread in Japan after World War II, however, the necessity for paving the streets and building sewage systems became urgent. These were conveniences that permitted a sophisticated, civilized way of life, but as environmentalists have pointed out, they do interfere with the natural functioning of the ecosystem. Rather, streets should be paved in such a way that rainwater can permeate back into the ground; if waste water from septic tanks is likewise restored to the earth, the functioning of the ecosystem will be properly maintained.

The Arithmetic of Form

Architectural space may be created in two ways: by addition and by subtraction. In some kinds of sculpture you start with nothing and create a work of art by adding on clay, bit by bit. In other kinds you start with a block of stone or wood and hew it down, discarding unnecessary parts until the desired form takes shape. Likewise, there is one kind of architectural space that is created centrifugally, ordering the space from the inside out—this may be called architecture by addition. And there is another kind in which the space is created centripetally—by subtraction. The distinction depends on the relationship between the whole and the parts: whether you start with the parts or with the whole. Examples of the former may be found in the works of Finnish architect Alvar Aalto, and among those of the latter type is the famous apartment building, the Unité d'Habitation by Le Corbusier. In Japan, examples of the former may be found in the traditional *sukiya* architecture; of the latter, the Tokyo Metropolitan Government office designed by Tange.

The essential difference between the works of these architects has to do with content and form, and how the decision as to which shall be given priority in creating space has been handled. The Unité apartment building is the epitome, if I may exaggerate a bit, of a type of structure that gives overwhelming attention to exterior proportions and architectural balance, with the content simply "stuffed" into the interior of the created architectural space.

In 1954, when I visited Paris after a year of study in the United States, I went to Le Corbusier's office. The architect was not there that day, but I was shown his studio. Strewn over the table were sketches, presumably by Le Corbusier himself, that looked like pictures of architectural prototypes. They seemed practically image sketches, and I remember wondering how he could turn out so many drawings of architectural form without knowing what kind of building he would be designing. Perhaps they were equivalent to the image sketches that sculptors often draw as ideas come to mind. Still, sculpture does not incorporate any function for living, a fact which sets it apart from architecture.

Later, I went to see Le Corbusier's Unité d'Habitation in Marseilles for myself. I will never forget my feeling of amazement and surprise. Seen from a distance, the proportions of the whole were truly splendid. The strong assertion of the materials in the powerful pilotis supports and the exposed concrete exterior was impressive, the deeply incised fenestrations and bright colors of the fittings striking. I felt as if I were seeing the three-dimensional embodiment of the sketches that had littered Le Corbusier's studio, the realization of a painting by, say, Mondrian.

Then I was shown inside. I had heard from the prominent Japanese architect Kunio Maekawa that Le Corbusier seldom paid visits to the sites of his buildings under construction; his concern was mainly with the conceptual design. And so it seemed. The interior treatment of detail was quite rough. Inside one of the apartments, I was even more surprised by the cramped, crude proportions of the space. Each apartment was 4.19 meters wide and about five times that long. How could anyone live in such elongated space, I wondered. We have such long, narrow town-houses in Kyoto, but they have small inner gardens and back gardens for each unit that make them liveable. The Unité was a perfect example of a design that begins with a well-proportioned, attractive whole and attends to the parts as an afterthought. I felt as if the building were a gigantic work of sculpture, and I understood why Le Corbusier was so impressed by the Parthenon.

Later, I visited Chandigarh, the capital complex designed by Le Corbusier for the Indian state of Punjab. This time it was the immense distances between the buildings that caught me by surprise. The project was like a huge sculpture garden, the image sketches on Corbusier's table many hundreds of times larger in scale, and totally oblivious to the harsh climate of the country. The buildings of the Chandigarh capital, each with its own explicit exterior form, were scattered over the site in positions determined by geometric relationship. They represented excellent examples of architecture constructed by subtraction from an exterior outline.

Unlike sculpture, architecture is intended to house interior space for human use or habitation. It is unnatural to predetermine the exterior form at the drawing board. I believe that architecture must by definition be designed after thorough analysis of the functions it is to house; exterior appearance ought to be such that the content of a structure oozes from every joint. A priori image sketches may be justifiable in the case of monuments or towers that have little going on inside them—one-room religious architecture such as the Ronchamp cathedral in Paris also by Le Corbusier, or the Olympic Swimming Pool in Tokyo by Tange, where interior space is chiefly devoted to one immense hall and minor errors in planning or details will not obstruct function. They are less appropriate for buildings for human habitation.

The same with hospitals. When architect Paul Rudolph, a leading light in American architecture some time ago, learned that I was designing a municipal hospital, he expressed some surprise. Architects like himself and Le Corbusier, he said, would probably never design a hospital even if requested, because detail is so important and there is so little freedom to exercise creativity in exterior form in such buildings. Indeed, Le Corbusier never did build a hospital, but Alvar Aalto did. A masterpiece among the early works of the Finnish architect is a tuberculosis sanatorium located in Paimio, a work that was acclaimed at the time as marking the beginning of modern architecture (fig. 16).

The reason I have singled out the architecture of Aalto is that he seems to create his designs by addition, not subtraction. His later works include an asymmetrically shaped church and an irregularly shaped auditorium (fig. 17). He is not the least concerned with module, proportion, or tidiness of geometrical form as Le Corbusier conceived them. In fact, one gets the impression that each necessary element of content is added on one after another. When you see the silhouettes of Aalto's works against the evergreen forests in their Finnish settings and observe the easy harmony between the content of building and surrounding landscape, you experience a warming sense of humanity and fulfillment.

In Le Corbusier's architecture the outlines are distinct, and all factors that might obstruct or blur their clarity are considered hindrances. In Alvar Aalto's architecture, on the other hand, the forest background is a desirable, necessary context, which makes all the more attractive the structure's outline (fig. 18). It reminds one of the Katsura and the Shugakuin detached palaces in Kyoto, where the buildings would not be complete without the surrounding gardens (fig. 19). By contrast, Le Corbusier's architecture is self-centered, requiring huge spaces, as in Chandigarh, so that it can be seen uninterrupted from a distance.

Some years ago, on a summer day, I climbed the Acropolis for the first time. There stood the Parthenon, its proud 2,000-year-old profile bathed in the intense brilliance of the Aegean sun. At first I was astonished at the world of unrelieved stone that met my eyes. Everything, from the pathway leading up the hill, its smoothed and rounded contours testifying to the passage of untold millions, to the gables of the Parthenon, was marble. Considering the transportation methods of ancient times, it made sense to build the structure from materials close at hand. No doubt the precisely chiseled marble columns and beams that form the Parthenon were made from blocks quarried nearby, as indeed, they seemed to rise organically out of the body of the hill itself.

There was not a tree in sight, and in the bright sunshine there was no ambiguity. Everything was cast in strong contrast, light or shadow, convex or concave, space or substance. The play of sunlight also colored the friezes, reliefs, and the fluting of the columns with impressive effect. The construction of this building in-

Fig. 16. Paimio sanitorium by Alvar Aalto; view of front and plan (*right top*).

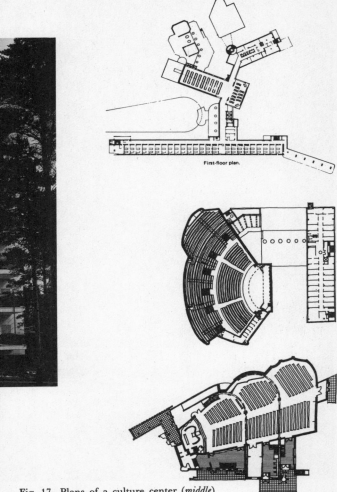

First-floor plan.

Fig. 17. Plans of a culture center (*middle*) and church (*bottom*) by Aalto.

Fig. 18. University building in a forest landscape, Otaniemi, Finland, by Aalto.

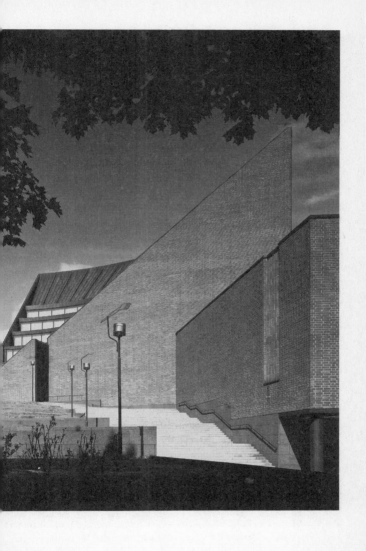

Fig. 19. Katsura Detached Palace building, concealed by shrubbery.

corporated the most up-to-date technology and know-how of the times—the use of entasis, the subtle arching of the horizontal members used to prevent the impression of sag. Whether seen by people atop a distant hill or by visitors standing right in front of it, the Parthenon appeared perfectly balanced and finely proportioned. This, I realized, was the prototype of the frontality and symmetry that is basic to European architecture (fig. 20). It is only when you come close enough to touch it that you are brought back to earth: this marvelous monument is actually nothing but a structure of cold stones piled up with unusual skill (fig. 21). This was architecture meant to be seen from afar—not near.

On subsequent trips to Greece, I gradually learned to appreciate how the strong sunlight served to highlight the beauty of the structure's exterior proportions rather than to draw attention to the texture of the materials. I visited Greece only once in the wintertime. It happened to be a gray, dreary day with drizzling rain, rare in Greece. I did not climb the Acropolis, for I was loathe to find the beautiful proportions of the Parthenon, so regal in clear weather, reduced to an amorphous mass of stone in the shadowless light of a rainy day. In architecture meant to be seen from afar, in form by subtraction, sharply defined features, sharply cut lines, frontality, symmetry, and lucidity are extremely important. Here, in ancient Grecian architecture, is the origin of the dualistic clarity of Western architecture as a whole.

Fig. 20. The Parthenon

Fig. 21. The Parthenon, close-up.

One can be impressed with the beautiful form and balance of a structure with an even simpler form—the pyramids in Egypt. The total planning, which dates back a few thousand years, was utterly meticulous. The Giza, for instance, was designed so that one side of the base would be exact, at 230 meters, and the height would be 146 meters. North, south, east, and west were taken into account, and the isosceles triangles had been tilted to $51°50'35''$ degrees so that they appear like equilateral triangles when seen from the ground. Over two million stones were transported and put into place systematically. At the time of construction, the white stone surface would have stood out in the brown desert all around it.

As one approaches the pyramid, however, the huge surface is revealed to be rough; with many stones stolen or fallen off, the effect is quite unbeautiful. The monument had been constructed from an architectural plan based on the whole, which is characteristic of the desert, dry with no trees. Had there been greater variability in the Egyptian environment—with need to add parts to the whole—the well-balanced, perfectly planned pyramids would never have been built (fig. 22).

By contrast, the first thing one notices about the traditional buildings of Japan are their relatively diminutive proportions, asymmetry, and modest facades, often deliberately hidden in the surrounding shrubbery (fig. 23). Upon close inspection, one sees that great attention has been given to the grain of

Fig. 22. Egyptian pyramid.

Fig. 23. Asymmetrically designed entrance to a Japanese dwelling.

the wood, its carefully smoothed texture, and the precision of its joints and interlocking timbers. Each such feature demonstrates a beauty in irregularity that originates from an inner—hidden—viewpoint; together they stand in sharp contrast to the beauty of proportions meant to be seen from a distance.

In fact, one discovers the real beauty of Japanese architecture not in bright, dazzling sunlight, but in dim candlelight or in the mellow illumination of a paper-covered lantern, and not from afar, but by drawing close to it and savoring the fragrance and the feel of wood and *tatami*. Even in our present society, these are the qualities that Japanese treasure most.

The Japanese aesthetic draws its inspiration from the subtle changes of the four seasons. The climate is characterized by considerable rainfall, and the wet and damp casts its spell over everything. Mist and moisture soften the lines and the contrasts between things and people, blurring shapes and obscuring the clear recognition of back or front, right side or left. The language is filled with terms that define the nuances and specific qualities of particular atmospheric states. There are *harugasumi* (spring mists), *asamoya* (morning mists), *samidare* (early summer rains), *baiu* (long, continuous rains of summer), *rin-u* (continuous rains), *yūdachi* (sudden evening downpour), *raiu* (thunderstorms), and as many terms again for the kinds of snow that fall.

Japanese also has special literary forms of words for

the colors of the sky and for the moon in different seasons. The heavy humidity in summer nourishes the lush growth of vegetation, which left untended can in no time literally envelop a low, traditional-style dwelling, obliterating its outlines. In the midst of this lush environment, any attempt at grand symmetry, proud frontality, or exterior symbolism is doomed. The aesthetic of Japan's climate thus came to be characterized by ambiguity and irregularity.

Let me now go back and take another look at the column in classical Greek architecture. Buildings were composed of columns and horizontal beams of stone, as roof construction methods using the arch, vault, and dome had not yet been introduced. Roofs were made of wood. What then was the significance of the largely decorative use of well-proportioned Corinthian orders with acanthus leaf motifs or scroll-capped Ionic orders in the design of the meeting point between stone columns and stone beams? Fritz Baumgart says that in terms of form, interior space did not play a very important role in Greek architecture.[14] It is possible that these decorative heads of columns were closely related to the exterior-oriented sense—the frontality and symbolism—of Greek architecture. Moreover, these Greek temples are built with the gable at the front.

In Japan, gable-fronted architecture is rare, except for temples and shrines, such as those of the *taisha-zukuri* style, typified by the main building at Izumo Shrine built two thousand years ago. Even this main building is not truly symmetrical, for the entrance

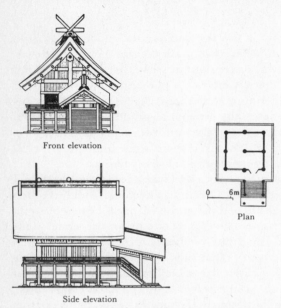

Front elevation

Plan

0   6 m

Side elevation

Fig. 24. Izumo Shrine, front elevation, side elevation, plan.

is located to the right of the central column. Far
from emphasizing frontality, it appears deliberately to
offset the building's balance (figs. 24, 25). In Rothenburg, the gables of the houses, each with its own
distinctive identity, face squarely on the street, endowing the townscape with a proud, outward-looking
visage. In Kyoto, by contrast, the low, two-storied
townhouses are built with their gables hidden from the
street, and the townscape impresses one as secretive
and reticent.

Fig. 25. Izumo Shrine, main building.

In the history of Buddhist architecture in Japan, there are three main styles: *tenjikuyō*, *karayō*, and *wayō*. The distinctive features of these styles are the bearing block and bracket arm supports for the long eaves. These bracket systems played an important role, not only dynamically as supports, but aesthetically in each different style. Although one might be tempted to correlate these bracket complex styles with the Greek orders, it is wise to keep in mind that they are less important as elements of external decoration—as are Ionic, Doric, or Corinthian columns—than as a rational, dynamic means of support suited to the functional Japanese aesthetic. They are tucked tidily and unprepossessingly into dim recesses under the massive roofs of temples or shrines. From a distance they are completely out of view, but close at hand, it is the technology and aesthetic of the bracket complexes that we find most impressive (figs. 26, 27). Even Japan's large-scale Buddhist structures, in contrast to Greek architecture, are in fact designed to be viewed close-up.

In architecture intended to be viewed from afar, emphasis is placed on grasping the whole exterior, while that intended to be seen at close quarters gives more attention to the detail and texture of each part. One is not necessarily superior or inferior to the other, but the difference highlights the contrasts between the culture that emerged in Japan's peculiar climate and that which grew out of the Greek tradition of Western civilization.

Fig. 26. Bracket complexes of the Great South Gate, Tōdaiji, Nara.

Fig. 27. Bracket complexes of the Great Buddha Hall, Tōdaiji.

Architecture constructed by addition begins with the parts and proceeds from there to form an external order. Architecture that is built by subtraction starts with a whole, which is then subdivided to form an inner order of parts. In considering such hierarchical orders, look at Arthur Koestler's idea of the *holon*, which comes from the Greek word *holos*, meaning whole.[15]

Koestler tells the story of two watchmakers named Bios and Mecos who lived in Switzerland. Each made watches assembled from a thousand parts. Mecos made each watch by setting the parts one by one. Bios made his by first putting together groups of ten or so parts and then assembling the ten or so groups to produce a finished watch. When his work was interrupted or if he dropped a part on the floor, Mecos had to go back and start from scratch. Bios did not have to start all over again, and if he was interrupted just before completion, he only had to repeat a maximum of nine steps in the assembly process. Imagine if a watch were made of a thousand pieces and there were one interruption for every one hundred pieces. Under these circumstances Mecos would take four thousand times the time consumed by Bios to produce the same amount, and to do what Bios could accomplish in one year, Mecos would need eleven years.

Koestler notes that when a complex order evolves from a simple order, the evolution takes place at a faster pace in the existence of a stable intermediate form, compared to when there is none. He says, further, that the primary universal characteristic of hierarchy is the relativity and indistinctness of the words "part" and "whole." So obvious is this that it escapes our attention. The word "part," as we generally use it, signifies something piecemeal or incomplete, something whose existence is meaningless alone. A "whole" is something complete in itself that requires no further addition. In fact, however, such absolute wholes and parts do not exist. The "whole" organisms or bodies in society are actually "sub-wholes," intermediate entities that are parts in a multi-level hierarchy that grows increasingly complex. Depending on your viewpoint, each entity has the characteristics of a "whole" as well as of a "part." This is what Koestler called a *holon*.[16]

This idea of the *holon* can be applied to the formative process of architecture or of the city. One house, for instance, is a complete "whole" for the person who lives there, but it is also a "part" of the group of houses that form a distinct community. Still, it is not *just* a part, but in truth a stable intermediate form called a "sub-whole" that is a necessary element in the hierarchy leading from single houses to the complex city. The "sub-whole" has a certain universality that is linked to a "sub-whole" of a higher order. The concept of a *holon* contains an element that is common to the whole, like a gene. Just as a branch of a tree or a fragment of a rock possesses qualities that suggest to us something about the whole, individual buildings in a city have shared characteristics that contribute to the higher order of the city as a whole. If every structure in a given area is composed of entirely heterogeneous elements, it becomes extremely difficult to build a community of a higher order that encompasses them all.

The architecture by addition I mentioned earlier is not really a matter of simple addition, but a process based on the selection of common factors influenced by the hidden order. The concept of the "sub-whole" can be found in the essential principles of Japanese architecture and of its cities, just as in Alvar Aalto's architecture by addition. Architecture by subtraction, I believe, does not accommodate the idea of "sub-whole," for the totality asserts itself above all else.

The architecture of Tokyo—as well as other cities in Japan—has much in common with the ontogeny of living organisms; they are constantly changing in accordance with their content and function. And though they may lack some completeness or singularity of form in the artistic sense, they are endowed with "redundancy." Within the chaos, we are beginning to recognize that there is a kind of hidden order. We need to be more aware of the "sub-whole"—the *holon* —in individual buildings, in particular townscapes. Tokyo's architecture and townscape, which seems chaotic at first sight, can offer an object lesson in Koestler's theory.

Chapter 4

Tokyo: A City Apart

Reflections in Paris

At this writing, I am sitting in a garret room of a hotel located on one corner of the Saint-Germain-des-Près quarter of Paris. I am here thinking about the architecture of Tokyo while actually shut up within the walls of one of the masonry structures of a European city. From the tiny balcony in front of the window of my room, I can see the high-rise buildings of Montparnasse in the distance against the gray winter sky. The Café Flore and the Café Aux Deux Magots are nearby.

I am always struck by the clean lines of the Paris townscape: stately masonry buildings in well-disciplined alignment on both sides of broad boulevards, even rows of well-trimmed trees. The pervasive sense of order is perhaps all the more evident because the trees are completely barren of leaves in this season. I have visited Paris many times, and always it is the same, with its serene stone walls, cobbled streets paved with genuine stone, and colorfully clad citizens bustling to and fro.

What is the secret of this city's attractiveness? And is its beauty really eternal, as the Parisians boast? How will Paris, completed in the nineteenth century, change between now and the dawn of the twenty-first century? Or will it not change at all? I wonder about these questions, inevitably comparing Paris to my hometown Tokyo, which, far from being an eternal city, is known for its several rebirths and ever-changing face. In fact, these two cities are as different in concept as they are in appearance.

First of all, there is the matter of architectural orientation: the distinction between "outside" (exterior) and "inside" (interior). An exterior is a man-made form, and an interior is essentially the content of that form. Now, from what I see in Paris and from what I know of Tokyo, one of my first observations is that form has historically—at least since the Renaissance—had precedence in the West, while in Japan content—the inside of the buildings—has always been given greater attention. For instance, the subdivisions of Western architectural history are delineated by the distinctive forms of architecture of each period. The different eras are discriminated chiefly by the form and exterior expression of architecture: Egyptian, Greek, and Roman, early Christian, Romanesque, Gothic, Renaissance, Baroque, and Neo-classic.

In Japanese architectural history, by contrast, the most important concerns are how the architecture is used and the historical periods in which buildings are constructed. Take, for instance, the Hokkedō at Tōdai-ji, also called Sangatsudō (fig. 28). This temple building, one of the most important historical mon-

Fig. 28. Sangatsudō temple hall, left portion built
in the Nara period, 9th century; right portion
added during the Kamakura period, 13th century.

uments of the Nara period (710–794), has a hipped
and gabled roof that was added in the Kamakura
period (1185–1336) to the hip roof of its main section,
built in the Nara period. Even under close observation, however, the overall form of the building is so
well integrated that unless one is previously aware of

what part was built in what period, he might never notice that an addition had been made to the original structure. If you look carefully at the area where the two parts of the building join, you will observe some differences in the bracket complexes under the eaves that presumably reflect the style of the times, but they seem trivial in view of the unity and coordination of the roof (fig. 29).

Architectural historian Minoru Ōoka tells us that the Hokkedō, which now forms one structure, was originally made up of two separate buildings with a rain trough affixed between them.[17] As far as the interior space is concerned, however, it has always formed a single hall (fig. 30). The two sections built in the Nara and Kamakura periods blend together so harmoniously that in terms of either architectural design or architectural form, the present plan showing the Hokkedō as a single structure is superior to the original two-structure plan.

The chief focus of attention of such styles of architecture as *shinden zukuri* (the style of residence of the Heian aristocracy) or *buke zukuri* (style of residence of the Kamakura warrior class) is not so much form as defined by exterior appearance as content, the lifestyle and functions that took place inside.

There are various forms of architecture in Japan corresponding to each historical period, but they do not qualify as architectural style per se. I believe it is more accurate to associate each with a particular lifestyle, that is, a given way—content—of life. For example,

Fig. 29. Sangatsudō, point at which the two independently constructed roofs join.

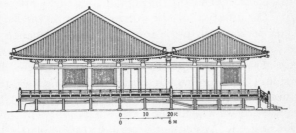

Fig. 30. Sangatsudō, original elevation from the Nara period.

shinden zukuri, often treated as a style, is more precisely the dwelling type of a particular stratum of Heian period (794–1185) society—the aristocracy. Structures of this type centered around a *shinden*, the quarters occupied by the head of the household, and had wings extending from the east and west ends, the whole usually facing a pond on the south side. The house was often connected to a fishing pavilion on the edge of the pond by a bridge-like walkway. In these *shinden zukuri* (fig. 31) houses, as described in romantic detail in *The Tale of Genji* (fig. 32), gentlemen courted ladies with poetry and plaintive songs strummed on the lute (*biwa*).

Buke zukuri flourished during the Kamakura period, beginning with the ascendency of the first of the country's warrior leaders, Minamoto no Yoritomo, in the late twelfth century and developing through the Muromachi age, lasting through the mid-sixteenth century. The lifestyle of the warrior class of medieval Japan, in contrast to the somewhat effete elegance of the court aristocracy, was rugged and practical. In place of the isolated pavilion-like rooms connected by corridors that were characteristic of *shinden zukuri*, the warrior's homes were more centralized, like the defense-oriented castle (fig. 33).

During the Momoyama period (1568–1603), the many provincial lords (*daimyō*) who governed the country built castles as the headquarters of their domains, each demonstrating a unique local flavor. The

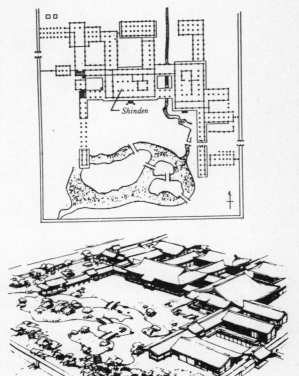

Shinden

Fig. 31. Typical *shinden zukuri* dwelling, plan and perspective.

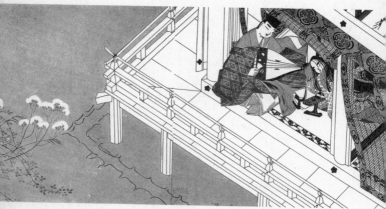

Fig. 32. Scroll, scene from *Genji monogatari*.

residences of wealthy members of the warrior class were described as *shoin zukuri*, and here again the term evokes not so much an architectural style as a way of life. The name comes from the inclusion of a *shoin*, or study, and these houses were decorated with a vigorous masculine taste that is completely Japanese and uninfluenced by the architecture of other countries.

With the advent of the Edo period (1603–1868), imaginative, ostentatious forms began to give way to a preference for restrained simplicity typified by tea

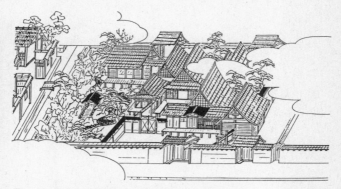

Fig. 33. Typical *buke zukuri* dwelling, perspective.

ceremony architecture. This aesthetic architectural taste led to the development of the so-called *šukiya zukuri*, of which the Katsura and Shugakuin detached palaces are outstanding examples. With their slender posts and cypress bark-covered roofs, they blend harmoniously into their landscaped settings. From this form developed the ultimate in the refined simplicity of tea ceremony architecture (figs. 34, 35).

There are, of course, distinctive forms of bracket complexes, ceiling designs, and roof truss constructions that can be identified as styles. *Wayō* (original

Fig. 34. Katsura Detached Palace, exemplifying the *sukiya* style.

Fig. 35. Tea ceremony room of Sa-an, Gyokurin-in, Daitokuji, Kyoto.

Japanese style), *tenjikuyō* or *daibutsuyō* (Sung Chinese style), and *karayō* (Zen style) are examples. But their characteristics are found in relatively inconspicuous parts of the buildings—what we might call *yin* features—such as supporting bracket complexes under the roof's elongated eaves. In contrast, the elements that display the style of a Western building are those that govern its external appearance—say, a row of Grecian columns—which is to say the dominant, *yang*, parts of the building.

In the 1920s, with the advent of modern architecture, there emerged in Japan a trend towards integration of form and content, based on the idea that external appearance should be a faithful reflection of internal functions and structure. Under the slogan "form follows function," this movement sought to eliminate all the decorative elements of architecture that had once been conceived of as central in the history of Western architectural style. In its avoidance of symmetry and frontality, attention to harmony with the natural landscape, and tendency to dispense with any unnecessary decoration, traditional Japanese architecture coincided with the spirit of the modern architecture movement that arose in the West. But it differed in that it had always been characterized by an open structure conducive to fluidity between the inside and the outside. For this reason, faithful expression of function and structure came quite naturally.

Philip Johnson's glass house built after the war in the Connecticut suburb of New Canaan is a candid expression of both interior functions and structure. The fluidity of inner and outer space achieved by its large glass walls and framework of steel posts and beams, so resembling the lines of a painting by Mondrian, was a declaration of liberation from conventional styles of architecture. An exhibition of Japanese traditional architecture held around the same time at the Museum of Modern Art in New York revealed that the principles that were being sought in the West by the modern architecture movement had been present in traditional Japanese wood-construction architecture for more than three hundred years. Many Americans became enamored of the wall-less spaces found in such buildings as the Old Shoin at Katsura Detached Palace or the Bōsen-no-ma of the Kohōan at Daitokuji (fig. 36). For the first time in Western architectural history, buildings began to be more than mere symbols of style or art; they became closely bound up with technology and content, what were called vessels for living.

The modern architecture movement, however, has failed to give sufficient attention to humane and natural environments, and is now groping for new directions. A new trend is emerging under the aegis of post-modernism that again places some priority on the form and external expression of architecture as opposed to content. An internationally known example is Michael Graves' Portland, Oregon, City Hall with its striking facade. Another is the Tsukuba Center Building designed by Japanese architect Arata Isozaki, in which the pavement pattern created for the Piazza

Campidoglio in Rome by Michelangelo is reproduced in reverse for the central plaza (figs. 37, 38).

Neither the Portland City Hall facade nor the Tsukuba Center pavement are related to the content of their respective buildings; they are examples of the reappearance of past styles and decorative elements rejected by modern architecture that are once more giving form and expression dominance over content. With the emergence of the modern architecture movement, Western architecture moved away from its history of styles, seeking an integration of form and content. Architects around the world again began to bring form back into the limelight, but their creations were not so much neo-classic revivals of form in the strict sense as what might be called a humorous neo-mannerism.

As is apparent in Western architecture, particularly from the time of the Renaissance onward, style is closely associated with the external expression of a building as determined by its composition as well as with such concepts as symmetry, frontality, symbolism, and monumentality. In post-Renaissance Italy there was a strong tendency to approach architecture as within the existing context of the city. It was as if the content were insignificant as long as the form and expression were clear and symmetric; it hardly mattered that the street and the building behind it were irregular and crooked.

It is similarly so with the buildings of Andrea Palladio, the Venetian Renaissance architect. Standing

Fig. 36. Bōsen-no-ma, Kohōan, Daitokuji, Kyoto.

Fig. 37. Piazza Campidoglio, Rome; pavement pattern designed by Michelangelo.

Fig. 38. Tsukuba Center building, with reversed Piazza Campidoglio; pavement pattern designed by Arata Isozaki.

before the San Giorgio Maggiore Cathedral in the Piazza San Marco (fig. 39), one is struck with its perfect symmetrical balance and frontality. This building was completed after Palladio's death, and it is believed that the proportions of the pillars do not follow his original design. The facade consists of two overlapped gables in the classical style, but the four staunch pilasters topped with Corinthian orders seem to have been added more for the sake of frontality and symmetry than as support for the eaves. The beauty of this facade, analyzed by using diagonal lines, for instance, is in the proportions of its elevation. But like the facades of so many other Venetian cathedrals, this one appears from the side of the building to be tacked on like a mask. I was rather shocked to find that the sides and backs of these buildings were finished with much less care than the fronts, often using completely different materials. My favorite view of the San Giorgio Maggiore Cathedral is from a distance out in the lagoon (fig. 40). From this perspective, the frontality of the facade is projected with almost unreal force, reminding me of the eerie surrealism of a holographic image.

Palladio also renovated the outer face of the Basilica Palladiana in the ancient Roman city of Vicenza, applying a Baroque style facade to the former Palazzo de la Ragione built in the medieval age. By adding equalsized cerulean arches between the irregularly spaced

Fig. 39. San Giorgio Maggiore Cathedral, Venice.

Fig. 40. View of San Giorgio Maggiore Cathedral from the lagoon.

columns of the original building and adjusting the breadth of the walls on either side of each arch to absorb the unevenness, he created an arcade of unity and regularity that dominates the townscape. The faces of the buildings surrounding the Piazza San Marco in Venice were likewise refurbished by changing only the facades. One cannot but think how, from the time of the Renaissance, European cities had been treated like stage settings, the frontality of architecture used, with the superficiality of two-dimensional drawings, to create attractive townscapes. How different from Tokyo, from all of Japan, where the emphasis has been on the functional, practical concerns relating to interior space.

But back to Paris, which is today the result of a drastic urban renewal plan undertaken by Haussmann under Napoleon III. What the city needed, they thought at the time, was a system of straight streets providing unobstructed views of the fine symmetrical and frontal buildings that stood at the heads of streets and the monuments located in piazzas at key intersections. The opera house designed by Charles Garnier rises high at the end of the Avenue de l'Opéra, resembling, as with the Madeleine which dominates the end of the Rue Royale, an immense tableau painting set up in the city. The visitor to Paris, moreover, need not actually go inside these buildings; a view of their outer form is enough to leave a lasting image.

The splendid exteriors of these buildings are, as I mentioned before, like so many false images projected by holography. We can well imagine the opera house and the Madeleine as holographic images made interchangeable by modern technology. Even more interesting, to me, is the sight of some buildings on which pictures of windows had been painted in order to preserve the symmetry of the designs. It appears that for the French, form and content need not necessarily coincide since inside and outside are clearly separated by stout walls; the beauty of a townscape is sustained to a large extent by the form. (Parisians, moveover, do not hang out their washing or bedding from windows or verandas, perhaps because of an instinctive desire to preserve the picturesque quality of the townscape.)

I am reminded of something a Polish architect friend once told me. After the war, the architecture in central Warsaw was restored to the exact original state, according to scale drawings based on actual measurements done before the bombings. Important exterior ornaments, which had been taken down for safekeeping before the war began, were put back into place. While the interior facilities of the buildings were greatly modernized, the external appearance of buildings was the same, and, he said, would always be the same.

This, too, is alien to Japanese thinking. The idea of the transience of things is deeply embedded in

Japanese culture, and one tends to emphasize the essence of things, rather than their material reality. An example is Ise Shrine, which has been rebuilt every twenty years since the eighth century. These regular rebuildings were suspended for a period of about 120 years beginning at the time of the Ōnin Wars (1467) when the country was torn by struggles between petty warlords. Once the rebuilding was resumed, they continued as before, the latest and sixtieth carried out in 1979.

As historian Daniel Boorstin observed in a lecture entitled "The Japanese Conquest of Time: The Arts of Renewal," to the Architectural Institute of Japan, attitudes toward time are quite different in Japan and the West. In the West, where nature was perceived as hostile, builders made structures of stone that could endure almost to eternity in a human attempt to deny mortality. The Japanese, by contrast, sought to live in coexistence with nature. To them, time was not something to be overcome by struggle; it was, rather, to be lived with through acceptance of its laws. The medium of architecture was wood, which embraced nature and yielded to time. Ise Shrine is not the real entity that existed in the Nara period, but a faithful reproduction of the original and timeless beauty of a structure that is still very much alive. It is different from the stone structures of the West, such as the Parthenon or the pyramids, which we view today as well-

Fig. 41. Ise Shrine, with one site cleared for rebuilding.

preserved ruins. At Ise Shrine, what is preserved is not the physical entity, but the expression and spirit of the architecture (figs. 41, 42).

The small towns along the Romantic Highway in southern Germany, which I have mentioned earlier, are particularly instructive in this regard. To a Japanese, the beautiful end-gables of the houses that line the road in such places as Rothenburg and

Fig. 42. Ise Shrine, main shrine.

Fig. 43. Kyoto townhouses lining the street horizontally.

Dinkelsbühl have a fantasy-like charm, each unique yet united with the others by a common aesthetic touch that never fails to charm. One is familiar with the traditional townscapes of places like Kyoto made up of townhouses built cheek-by-jowl along narrow streets, but these structures are constructed horizontally along the streets, their gables abutting one another (fig. 43)

Fig. 44. View of a typical Tokyo apartment building.

and out of sight as far as the townscape is concerned.

In southern German towns, the coloring of the gable ends and the fenestration of the windows are different for each house, yet well harmonized with their neighbors. The windowsills are fitted with planters filled with blossoming flowers. Such decoration of the exterior of buildings seems to represent a basic German emphasis on form. In Japan, by contrast, this conscious effort to contribute to a pleasant townscape does not seem to exist: you are more likely to find the verandas of houses and apartment buildings covered with bedding and laundry hung up to dry (fig. 44). (Admittedly, there are climatic reasons for this: bedding, which is laid directly on *tatami* floors, absorbs a great deal of body moisture and must be aired frequently. The lack of garden and yard space means that verandas and window ledges are the only places to hang up laundry.)

In examining the architectural forms of western Europe, one should note the geographical distribution of masonry construction. Masonry buildings are characterized by a gravity structure consisting of piled-up stones or bricks, a type of structure developed in areas of southern Europe—France, Italy, Spain and Greece—where the summers are dry with high temperatures and winters are relatively wet and cold. Masonry construction permits only relatively small—chiefly vertical—openings to be cut out of the body of the walls. Long horizontal apertures are generally not feasible because of the weight of the piled-up stones or bricks. Inside and outside, moreover, are clearly divided by the walls. The space inside the walls forms a secluded interior, and the exterior, completely apart from what goes on within, simply presents the exterior expression of the building. The weighty walls of masonry construction, in other words, represent solid, immovable boundaries between inside and outside that inevitably became the monuments of Western architectural history.

Similarly, it occurs to me that Paris is, above all, a city of form. Its streets are lined with forms and ornaments that do not necessarily reflect the life that goes on behind them. It is a city consciously made to look attractive and tidy, somewhat like a movie set. The walls of the buildings are neatly aligned, their heights equalized by building codes, and anything that might disturb the external order of the townscape—electric poles, wires or exterior advertising—is avoided. Symmetrical, frontally oriented buildings are surrounded with beautiful sculptures, fountains, gaslit lamps, and benches. As in a perspective painting of the Renaissance period, nothing is allowed to obstruct the vistas through the streets. Paris exists on the basis of a unified architectural principle. It is a beautiful city, or, shall I say, it was designed to be beautiful.

The Westerner may find nothing odd in this and would be dismayed at the lack of order or conformity that characterizes Tokyo, but in Japan there are elements other than form at work.

Meditations in the South Pacific

After spending a winter in the masonry buildings of Paris, I decided to seek out their architectural antithesis by visiting a hot and humid tropical country, and the kingdom of Tonga seemed a likely place. Made up of a chain of islands in the South Pacific, Tonga is a land of coconut trees and taro fields surrounded by clear, reef-filled waters, swept by cool sea breezes.

The sight of local folk stretched out beneath huge shade-giving trees along the beach and gazing out to sea is common (fig. 45). It is a peaceful, idyllic landscape—a real paradise. There are two distinct realms in this world—the shade beneath the trees, protected from the sun, and the rest of the land, nakedly exposed to the direct rays of the blazing tropical sun. Needless to say, the shade is vital to human existence. And from the interior of homes which afford Tongans this shade, there is a conspicuous absence of walls and other solid structures that might obstruct the view out. Indeed, walls would also block the cool sea breezes that bathe the islands.

This same method of coping with climatic conditions resulted in Japan in the open structure of dwellings. The key parts of such structures are the roof, with long eaves and pent extensions, and the floor, with *tatami* or board flooring. The poet Bashō once wrote, "The cool is my dwelling and my place of repose," and, indeed, the roof—man's substitute for the shelter of trees—and the floor became the key features of this kind of architecture. Walls are of relative unimportance (fig. 46).

As in Japan, the absence of masonry buildings in Tonga is not attributable to a lack of stones. Rather, the importance of ventilation for any abode in such a climate precludes all thought of piling up stones in order to create a dwelling. Masonry construction is

Fig. 45. In the shade, enjoying the sea breezes in Tonga.

Fig. 46. Shisendō, Kyoto; no walls obscure the view out of doors.

essentially wall-building; floors and roofs are added last. In hot, humid climates, the weight and thermal capacity of stone makes it unsuitable as a building material. Stone walls in whatever form simply do not suit the aesthetic sense or lifestyle of people whose favorite pastime is stretching out beneath the trees to enjoy refreshing breezes off the ocean. The shade under these trees is shifting and fluid, completely at the whim of the movements of the sun and wind, and people come and go with the heat of midday and the cool of evening.

The spaces created by Japanese post-and-beam architecture are likewise fluid and permeable, and the demarcation between exterior and interior is not clear. The ambiguity this creates in the outline of architecture is, I dare say, a key to Japanese culture influencing everything from the way people think to the quality of the townscape.

Consider now the townscape or urban scene that results from architecture built on the principle of ample ventilation. First of all, roofs and floors, providing shade and a place to enjoy the passing breezes, become the structural elements of greatest precedence; walls are practically unnecessary. Frontality and symmetry are of little importance. The classical ideal of a house was built for summer, and this remained the fundamental characteristic of residential design until after World War II. To cope with the hot summers and high humidity, it was crucial to arrange the rooms of a house on a north-south axis in order to make the best of natural ventilation. The spread of air-conditioning in recent years has made a great difference in architectural options, but Japanese in their lifestyle today still give precedence to the floor as opposed to the wall.

In beautifying Tokyo, then, Japanese must identify and apply methods of our own; we cannot rely on principles that govern cities in the West, like Paris. For all we may wish to tidy up the urban chaos that has grown up around us, we cannot change it overnight; it has emerged out of the workings of our nation's history, traditions, and our own attitudes toward living. The important thing is to go back to the fundamental qualities of the Japanese townscape, to draw out the good points and correct the unsightly parts wherever possible—in other words, to adopt a contextual approach. It would be out of the question to attempt to remake the present cities of Tokyo or Osaka into picturesque models like Paris or Rothenburg because of the fundamental differences in the treatment of content and form. We might, however, be able to improve the situation by finding ways to eliminate unsightly utility poles and lines, hanging billboards and advertising, and unattractive concrete fences or by encouraging people not to hang their wash from their front verandas.

The townscape built for shade and cool breezes has an ambiguity not found in the West, but it is endowed with a warmth and friendliness all its own. The crowded conditions and diverse architectural styles that coexist in Japanese cities may not be very attractive in form, but in content they embrace a certain hidden order. It is that hidden order that makes possible the vitality and prosperity of our cities today.

Chinese Architecture: More West Than East

Chinese architecture, one of the four major traditions of world architecture (along with European, Islamic, and Indian), has exerted a strong influence on both Japanese and Korean architectural history.[18] And so China was my next stop on this architectural journey.

The first wave of influence, coming to Japan from Six Dynasties, Sui, and Tang China, occurred during the Asuka and Nara periods (6th–8th centuries), with the introduction of Buddhism. Hōryūji temple in Nara stands as an example of wooden architecture built in the Asuka period.

Then followed a time during the Heian period when indigenous culture flourished. Later, during the Kamakura period, direct contacts were reestablished with the continent, and Japanese absorbed much again from Sung dynasty architectural styles, and the *tenjiku*-style great south gate of Tōdaiji was reconstructed.

In terms of the basic conceptualization of architecture, approach to planning and design, and attitudes toward architecture, Japan is not so closely associated with China as generally believed, however. Although the similarities between them are superficially quite striking, the fundamental treatment of architecture in the two cultures is poles apart. Japanese architecture is so different, I believe, as to make Chinese architecture seem to resemble that of Europe by contrast.

In considering a group of buildings, for example, one may conceive of them, as stated earlier, in one of two ways: by contemplating the whole to begin with or by starting with the "parts" that are to make up the whole. Of course, there are such things as a whole conceived in terms of its parts, and parts considered in terms of the whole, but in many cases, the emphasis in planning comes down heavily either on the whole or on the parts.

China's ancient city of Xian is a good example of planning in terms of the whole. Even today, the city is surrounded by walls (fig. 47), and roads leading from gates at the north, south, east, and west converge at the center, where a drum pavilion stands as a symbol of the city. The Han period planners of Xian some two millennia ago conceived of the city beginning with the whole and proceeding centripetally from the outside boundary, the castle walls. Even for our industrial society today, such a proposition would be considered quite a challenge; at the time, its construction must have been a monumental project.

The advanced technology developed through the building of such cities was brought to Japan by skilled craftsmen and artisans from both the Korean peninsula and the Chinese continent, and used in the construction of the Asuka-dera and Hōryūji temples and the Heijō and Heian capitals—Nara and Kyoto—over a thousand years ago. Surely the influx of culture from

Fig. 47. Xian, China, city wall.

the Asian continent was equal to, if not more dramatic than, the Meiji-period westernization of institutions and culture that brought about the building of such edifices as the famous modern Western-style Deer Cry Pavilion (Rokumeikan) along with the appearance of brick masonry in Japanese cities about one hundred years ago.

Any architectural concept that begins with the whole is imbued with the importance of symbolism, monumentality, and authoritarianism, and the resulting form therefore tends to favor symmetry, frontality, and a formal compositional and proportional aesthetic. Whole-oriented architecture was introduced to Japan, but was not compatible with Japanese tastes, and it inevitably yielded to the indigenous aesthetic, which favors asymmetry and restraint as well as harmony with the natural setting. The Heijō and Heian capitals, for instance, though patterned after models from China, do not have the imposing castle walls of Xian. The surrounding outer ring of fortifications, all largely formalistic, was not included in the Japanese version of the Chinese-style city,[19] and the absence of this outer boundary defining and controlling the whole undid the constraints of centripetalism, leaving room for spontaneity, gentleness, and diffuseness.

Consider the layout of the buildings at Hōryūji. The five-storied pagoda and the *kondō* (''golden'' or main image hall) are situated to the left and right, respectively, of the central axis originating at the middle gate (*chūmon*), thereby obstructing the symmetry of the whole (fig. 48). From the great south gate (*nandai-mon*), the pagoda and the *kondō* can be seen standing side by side through the middle gate. In comparison to the depth and symmetrical form of the layouts of older temples such as Asuka-dera and Shitennō-ji, this represents an unconventional (by Chinese standards), peculiarly Japanese aesthetic. Though seemingly under the influence of Chinese architecture in its form, this temple actually breaks all the rules, diverging from its models in the asymmetry of its plan, and in the detail of eave treatment, bracket complexes, and hand-rail design. The details are so skillfully executed that they may even be superior to those of the Chinese prototypes (fig. 49).

The period when this kind of temple compound was designed and constructed was the time when Japan was under the most direct influence of Chinese culture. In Chinese architecture both then and now, wood is the most basic medium of construction, and although stone and sun-dried brick are also used as building materials, the governing principles of wood structure design tend to be applied to these as well, wherever possible. It is also most common for the fronts of buildings to be oriented to the long side. Wood construction, the large, predominant roof, and side-front design are likewise typical of Japanese architecture and, in major respects, form a sharp contrast with the characteristic masonry construction, short eaves, and gable-fronted forms of Western architecture. While Japanese architecture remained

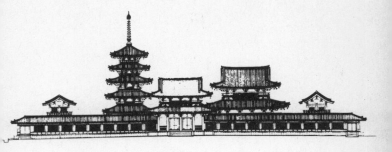

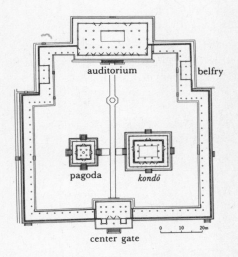

Fig. 48. Hōryūji, Nara, elevation and plan.

Fig. 49. Hōryūji, view from the front gate showing asymmetry of layout.

under the influence of Chinese civilization, its conceptualization was from the start stubbornly indigenous,
and this gradually evolved, as I have noted, into a
distinctive tradition culminating in the refinements of
the tea ceremony and *sukiya* architecture.

The tea ceremony cultivates an aesthetic that prizes
the unadorned, the imperfect and the incomplete.
Irregularity and asymmetry only emerge from a con-
vergence of parts; they are values difficult to integrate
in a whole-oriented view. The asymmetry of the
Japanese aesthetic reached its perfection in the treatment of plane surfaces: for example, the positioning of
the *tokonoma* alcove and windows in a room and the
treatment of ceilings in the modular spaces formed by
rooms the size of four-and-a-half, three, or two-and-
three-quarters *tatami* mats. Materials are often used in
their natural form for aesthetic effect: unbarked or
unplaned timbers, natural bamboo, reeds, rushes,
earth and chopped straw for walls, roofs of straw
thatch, miscanthus reed, or thin wood shingles.
Nowhere are there the bright colors used in the painted
decorations or azure tiles of Chinese architecture.

Examples of *sukiya* architecture are by now quite
well known even abroad, as are the Katsura and
Shugakuin detached palaces in Kyoto. The former
possesses a unique integrity, despite the fact that it is
composed of additions (the middle and new *shoin*) to
the original main building (old *shoin*) (fig. 50). What
makes this structure outstanding is that it presents not
only a marvelously unified whole, but also impressive

Fig. 50. Katsura Detached Palace, new, middle and old *shoin*.

precision in its detail, in the treatment of every joint. The beauty of such parts derives from the Japanese aesthetic that begins from parts, in turn endowing the whole with a detailed beauty.

The buildings at Katsura, built in the seventeenth century, show clearly how Japanese architecture broke away from Chinese influence, leading to a peculiarly Japanese conceptualization of the parts and the whole which understandably claimed the admiration of such Western architects as Bruno Taut and Walter Gropius. The garden of the Shugakuin Detached Palace, built for the Emperor Gomizuno-o (1611–1629), is designed in the promenade style with tea-ceremony huts positioned here and there on its sloped location at the foot of Mount Hiei.

It is interesting to compare the conceptualization of this complex with the splendid Yi He Yuan villa built by Chinese Emperor Xi Tai-hou in Beijing. For the latter, a huge artifical lake was dug to resemble the famous West Lake (Xi-hu) in Hang Zhou, and the earth thus removed was used to build the quite considerable hill called Wan Shou Shan. A series of pavilions was built leading from the foot all the way up to the summit. The idea of such a monumental project for creating an artificial lake and mountain, excavating and shaping the landscape to human designs, may not seem out of place in continental culture, but it is somewhat alien to the Japanese perception of nature (fig. 51).

China holds many unexpected wonders. One of the

Fig. 51. Yi He Yuan villa, Beijing.

things Japanese find startling is the quite different sense of scale, a remarkable example of which is the Great Wall. Originally built to help thwart the invasions of barbarian tribes, its proportions, again, are something completely beyond the conception of the inhabitants of a diminutive archipelago in the middle of the ocean. Faced with the need for devices to ward off enemies, Japanese would probably have resorted to something more piecemeal—the parts-oriented approach again—such as digging a moat, building a stockade or manufacturing arms. The Great Wall is above all a symbolic, perhaps overstated, monument of authority (fig. 52). If there is anything comparable to China's Great Wall or Egypt's pyramids in Japan, it is the ancient keyhole-shaped burial mound of Emperor Nintoku located in Nara prefecture. But, as is evident from an aerial view, this tumulus slopes elegantly and gently like a natural hill, and lacks all pretense of symbolism.

Modern Chinese architecture is very impressive in its presentation of the whole, but up close it often reveals a relative inattention to treatment of the parts. Even taking into account the fact that China is still in the process of modernization, it is hard for Japanese to understand how detail in contemporary Chinese architecture can be treated so clumsily. A modern hotel in Chongqing, for example, modelled after the historical Tian Tan Qinian-Dien temple, is an imposing display of the whole, with its symmetry, frontality, and brilliant color decorations. Close to and inside the

Fig. 52. The Great Wall of China.

building, however, one becomes less aware of its overall splendor, and rather disappointed to find the treatment of detail extremely rough (figs. 53, 54).

Why, I wonder, do the Chinese seek such symbolism of the whole and yet have such seeming disregard for the parts? From this point of view, too, I found my experience staying in the People's Hall in Xian unforgettable. Its indoor fixtures were rather shabby—there were various problems with doorknobs, lights and bathroom fixtures—yet on the outside there was a splendid string of colored bulbs illuminating the symmetrical outline of its great roof. In Japan, we are less conscious of the exterior image of buildings, and somewhat behind the times in the illumination of roof ridgelines or use of flood-lights, as so often seen in Europe, to display the symmetry and frontality of buildings at night.

Attention to detail in Japanese architecture, on the other hand, sometimes goes to the extreme. Perhaps there is a kind of levelling principle at work in Japanese culture according to which the completion of individual parts is expected to precede the presentation of the whole, even to the point of rejection of the whole. This is perhaps why the similarity with Chinese architecture only goes so far. Chinese architecture is designed to be viewed from afar, and in this respect it can be said to be more akin to the European and Greek traditions than it is to Japanese architecture. The distinction between Japanese and Chinese architecture, I would say, is in approach to the parts and the whole.

Fig. 53. New hotel in Chongqing.

As the twenty-first century nears, we are entering a
democratic age, in which total planning based on
whole-oriented conceptualization will be increasingly
ill-suited to the needs of urban development. No matter how troublesome it may seem, the parts-oriented
approach oriented to individual tastes and specific purposes must be given its due. We are entering a time
when individual fulfillment and distinctive tastes are
demanding priority. People are no longer willing to

Fig. 54. Tian Tan Qinian-Dien temple, Beijing.

submit quietly to the overriding interests of the whole but are asserting their demand for attention to the parts. This shift in values is already changing economic and political life, and it will no doubt affect the development of modern cities as well. The qualities of a city like Tokyo that is parts-oriented to begin with, although appearing chaotic and lacking any principle of order, may at last be appreciated in the coming age.

NOTES

1. Editorial Committee for the Handbook on Nutrition (ed.), *Eiyō handobukku* [Handbook on Nutrition] (Tokyo: Gihodō, 1974), Appendix, p. 1653.

2. Translation of *Tsurezuregusa* by G. B. Sansom, in *Anthology of Japanese Literature*, compiled and edited by Donald Keene (Tokyo: Charles E. Tuttle Co., 1955), pp. 233, 238.

3. Hirotarō Ōta, *Nihon kenchikushi josetsu* [An Introduction to the History of Japanese Architecture] (Tokyo: Shōkokusha, 1947), p. 37.

4. *See* Yoshinobu Ashihara, *The Aesthetic Townscape* (Cambridge, Massachusetts: The MIT Press, 1983).

5. Marcel Breuer, *Sun and Shadow* (New York: Dodd, Mead & Co., 1955), p. 32.

6. *See* the preface to the Japanese edition of *The Tao of Physics*, by Fritjof Capra (Tokyo: Kōsakusha, 1979), p. 340.

7. Jun'ichirō Tanizaki, *In'ei raisan* [In Praise of Shadows] (Tokyo: Chūōkoron-sha, 1975), p. 26.

8. Shōsaburō Kimura, *Kazoku no jidai: Yoroppa to Nihon* [The Era of the Family: Europe and Japan] (Tokyo: Shinchōsha, 1985), p. 46.

9. River Bureau, Japan Ministry of Construction (ed.), *Kaigan tōkei* [Statistics on the Coasts], 1985.

10. Benoit B. Mandelbrot, *The Fractal Geometry of Nature* (New York: W. H. Freeman & Co., 1983), p. 25.

11.   Roland Barthes, *L'Empire des Signes* (Genève: Editions d'Art Albert Skira, 1970).

12.   Mayumi Yoshinari, "Ransūkei ga umidasu bi no kōzō" [The Structure of Beauty Deriving from Random Figures], *Chūōkōron* (January 1985).

13.   Toyoyuki Sabata, *Suidō no bunka: Sei-ō to Nihon* [The Culture of Sewage and Water Supply] (Tokyo: Shinchōsha, 1983).

14.   Fritz Baumgart, *Stilgeschichte der Architektur* (Köln: Du-Mont Buchverlag, 1977).

15.   Arthur Koestler, *The Ghost in the Machine* (London: Hutchinson & Co., 1976), part III, chapter 3.

16.   *Ibid.*

17.   Minoru Ōoka, *Nihon kenchiku no ishō to gihō* [Design and Technique in Japanese Architecture] (Tokyo: Chūōkōron Bijutsu Shuppan, 1941), p. 32.

18.   Mitsuo Inoue, *Kenchikushi* [The History of Architecture] (Tokyo: Rikōtosho, 1953), p. 4.

19.   Hirotarō Ōta, *Nihon kenchikushi josetsu* [An Introduction to the History of Japanese Architecture] (Tokyo: Shōkokusha, 1947), p. 6.

INDEX

Page numbers in italics refer to illustrations.

CREDITS

The architect of Tokyo's landmark Sony Building, **Yoshinobu Ashihara** was educated at the University of Tokyo and in 1953 was awarded a master's degree in architecture from Harvard University. After working with Marcel Breuer in New York, he traveled widely in Europe on a Rockefeller grant.

Returning to Tokyo, Ashihara soon established his own architectural firm. His best-known works through the years include the National Museum of Japanese History, the Komazawa Olympic Gymnasium, the Dai-ichi Kangyō Bank's head office, the Japan Pavilion at Expo '67 in Montreal, and the Tokyo Metropolitan Symphony Hall.

Among other honors, he has received the Minister of Education's Arts Award, the Special Prize of the Architectural Institute of Japan, the Order of the Commendatore from the Italian government, and the Insignia of Commander of the Lion from the Finnish government. He was also appointed an Honorary Fellow of both the American and Australian Institutes of Architects. Ashihara held the post of president of the Architectural Institute of Japan from 1985 to 1986, and in 1991 he was cited by the Japanese government for cultural merit.

To his thriving architectural practice Ashihara has added teaching responsibilities at Hōsei University, Musashino Art University, and the University of Tokyo. He has been visiting professor at the University of New South Wales, the University of Hawaii, and Tianjin University in China.

Ashihara has written extensively on architecture, urban design, and culture. This is his third book to be published in English.